Washington Nationals 2020

A Baseball Companion

Edited by R.J. Anderson, Craig Goldstein and Bret Sayre

Baseball Prospectus

Craig Brown, Steven Goldman and David Pease, Consultant Editors
Robert Au, Harry Pavlidis and Amy Pircher, Statistics Editors

Copyright © 2020 by DIY Baseball, LLC.
All rights reserved

This book or any part thereof may not be reproduced or transmitted in any form or by any means, electronic or mechanical, including photocopying, recording, or by any information storage and retrieval system, without permission in writing from the publisher.

Limit of Liability/Disclaimer of Warranty: While the publisher and the author have used their best efforts in preparing this book, they make no representations or warranties with respect to the accuracy or completeness of the contents of this book and specifically disclaim any implied warranties of merchantability or fitness for a particular purpose. No warranty may be created or extended by sales representatives or written sales materials. The advice and strategies contained herein may not be suitable for your situation. You should consult with a professional where appropriate. Neither the publisher nor the author shall be liable for any loss of profit or any other commercial damages, including but not limited to special, incidental, consequential, or other damages.

Library of Congress Cataloging-in-Publication Data:
paperback
ISBN-13: 978-1-950716-22-7

Project Credits
Cover Design: Michael Byzewski at Aesthetic Apparatus
Interior Design and Production: Jeff Pease, Dave Pease
Layout: Jeff Pease, Dave Pease

Baseball icon courtesy of Uberux, from https://www.shareicon.net/author/uberux

Ballpark diagram courtesy of Lou Spirito/THIRTY81 Project, https://thirty81project.com/

Manufactured in the United States of America
10 9 8 7 6 5 4 3 2 1

Table of Contents

Statistical Introduction v

Part 1: Team Analysis

Washington Nationals: Where Are You Going, Where Have You Been? .. 3
    Jarrett Seidler, Scott Delp and Matthew Trueblood

Performance Graphs 7

2019 Team Performance 8

2020 Team Projections 9

Team Personnel 10

Nationals Park Stats 11

Nationals Team Analysis 13

Part 2: Player Analysis

Nationals Player Analysis 20

Nationals Prospects 105

Part 3: Featured Articles

The Baseball Is Juiced (Again) 119
    Robert Arthur

The Moral Hazard of Playing It Safe 123
    Craig Goldstein

Index of Names 129

Statistical Introduction

Sports are, fundamentally, a blend of athletic endeavor and storytelling. Baseball, like any other sport, tells its stories in so many ways: in the arc of a game from the stands or a season from the box scores, in photos, or even in numbers. At Baseball Prospectus, we understand that statistics don't replace observation or any of baseball's stories, but complement everything else that makes the game so much fun.

What stats help us with is with patterns and precision, variance and value. This book can help you learn things you may not see from watching a game or hundred, whether it's the path of a career over time or the breadth of the entire MLB. We'd also never ask you to choose between our numbers and the experience of viewing a game from the cheap seats or the comfort of your home; our publication combines running the numbers with observations and wisdom from some of the brightest minds we can find. But if you *do* want to learn more about the numbers beyond what's on the backs of player jerseys, let us help explain.

Offense

We've revised our methodology for determining batting value. Long-time readers of the book will notice that we've retired True Average in favor of a new metric: Deserved Runs Created Plus (DRC+). Developed by Jonathan Judge and our stats team, this statistic measures everything a player does at the plate–reaching base, hitting for power, making outs, and moving runners over–and puts it on a scale where 100 equals league-average performance. A DRC+ of 150 is terrific, a DRC+ of 100 is average and a DRC+ of 75 means you better be an excellent defender.

DRC+ also does a better job than any of our previous metrics in taking contextual factors into account. The model adjusts for how the park affects performance, but also for things like the talent of the opposing pitcher, value of different types of batted-ball events, league, temperature and other factors. It's able to describe a player's expected offensive contribution than any other statistic we've found over the years, and also does a better job of predicting future performance as well.

There's a lot more to DRC+'s story, and you can read all about it in greater depth near the end of this book.

Washington Nationals 2020

The other aspect of run-scoring is baserunning, which we quantify using Baserunning Runs. BRR not only records the value of stolen bases (or getting caught in the act), but also accounts for all the stuff that doesn't show up on the back of a baseball card: a runner's ability to go first to third on a single, or advance on a fly ball.

Defense

Where offensive value is *relatively* easy to identify and understand, defensive value is...not. Over the past dozen years, the sabermetric community has focused mostly on stats based on zone data: a real-live human person records the type of batted ball and estimated landing location, and models are created that give expected outs. From there, you can compare fielders' actual outs to those expected ones. Simple, right?

Unfortunately, zone data has two major issues. First, zone data is recorded by commercial data providers who keep the raw data private unless you pay for it. (All the statistics we build in this book and on our website use public data as inputs.) That hurts our ability to test assumptions or duplicate results. Second, over the years it has become apparent that there's quite a bit of "noise" in zone-based fielding analysis. Sometimes the conclusions drawn from zone data don't hold up to scrutiny, and sometimes the different data provided by different providers don't look anything alike, giving wildly different results. Sometimes the hard-working professional stringers or scorers might unknowingly inflict unconscious bias into the mix: for example good fielders will often be credited with more expected outs despite the data, and ballparks with high press boxes tend to score more line drives than ones with a lower press box.

Enter our Fielding Runs Above Average (FRAA). For most positions, FRAA is built from play-by-play data, which allows us to avoid the subjectivity found in many other fielding metrics. The idea is this: count how many fielding plays are made by a given player and compare that to expected plays for an average fielder at their position (based on pitcher ground ball tendencies and batter handedness). Then we adjust for park and base-out situations.

When it comes to catchers, our methodology is a little different thanks to the laundry list of responsibilities they're tasked with beyond just, well, catching and throwing the ball. By now you've probably heard about "framing" or the art of making umpires more likely to call balls outside the strike zone for strikes. To put this into one tidy number, we incorporate pitch tracking data (for the years it exists) and adjust for important factors like pitcher, umpire, batter and home-field advantage using a mixed-model approach. This grants us a number for how many strikes the catcher is personally adding to (or subtracting from) his pitchers' performance...which we then convert to runs added or lost using linear weights.

Framing is one of the biggest parts of determining catcher value, but we also take into account blocking balls from going past, whether a scorer deems it a passed ball or a wild pitch. We use a similar approach—one that really benefits from the pitch tracking data that tells us what ends up in the dirt and what doesn't. We also include a catcher's ability to prevent stolen bases and how well they field balls in play, and *finally* we come up with our FRAA for catchers.

Pitching

Both pitching and fielding make up the half of baseball that isn't run scoring: run prevention. Separating pitching from fielding is a tough task, and most recent pitching analysis has branched off from Voros McCracken's famous (and controversial) statement, "There is little if any difference among major-league pitchers in their ability to prevent hits on balls hit in the field of play." The research of the analytic community has validated this to some extent, and there are a host of "defense-independent" pitching measures that have been developed to try and extract the effect of the defense behind a hurler from the pitcher's work.

Our solution to this quandary is Deserved Run Average (DRA), our core pitching metric. DRA looks like earned run average (ERA), the tried-and-true pitching stat you've seen on every baseball broadcast or box score from the past century, but it's very different. To start, DRA takes an event-by-event look at what the pitchers does, and adjusts the value of that event based on different environmental factors like park, batter, catcher, umpire, base-out situation, run differential, inning, defense, home field advantage, pitcher role and temperature. That mixed model gives us a pitcher's expected contribution, similar to what we do for our DRC+ model for hitters and FRAA model for catchers. (Oh, and we also consider the pitcher's effect on basestealing and on balls getting past the catcher.)

It's important to note that DRA is set to the scale of runs allowed per nine innings (RA9) instead of ERA, which makes DRA's scale slightly higher than ERA's. The reason for this is because ERA tends to overrate three types of pitchers:

1. Pitchers who play in parks where scorers hand out more errors. Official scorers differ significantly in the frequency at which they assign errors to fielders.
2. Ground-ball pitchers, because a substantial proportion of errors occur on groundballs.
3. Pitchers who aren't very good. Better pitchers often allow fewer unearned runs than bad pitchers, because good pitchers tend to find ways to get out of jams.

Washington Nationals 2020

Since the last time you picked up an edition of this book, we've also made a few minor changes to DRA to make it better. Recent research into "tunneling"—the act of throwing consecutive pitches that appear similar from a batter's point of view until after the swing decision point–data has given us a new contextual factor to account for in DRA: plate distance. This refers to the distance between successive pitches as they approach the plate, and while it has a smaller effect than factors like velocity or whiff rate, it still can help explain pitcher strikeout rate in our model.

New Pitching Metrics for 2020

We're including a few "new" pitching metrics in the book for the 2020 edition, though unlike last year, these numbers may be a little bit more familiar to those of you who have spent some time investigating baseball statistics.

Fastball Percentage

Our fastball percentage (FB%) statistic measures how frequently a pitcher throws a pitch classified as a "fastball," measured as a percentage of overall pitches thrown. We qualify three types of fastballs:

1. The traditional four-seam fastball;
2. The two-seam fastball or sinker;
3. "Hard cutters," which are pitches that have the movement profile of a cut fastball and are used as the pitcher's primary offering or in place of a more traditional fastball.

For example, a pitcher with a FB% of 67 throws any combination of these three pitches about two-thirds of the time.

Whiff Rate

Everybody loves a swing and a miss, and whiff rate (WHF) measures how frequently pitchers induce a swinging strike. To calculate WHF, we add up all the pitches thrown that ended with a swinging strike, then divide that number by a pitcher's total pitches thrown. Most often, high whiff rates correlate with high strikeout rates (and overall effective pitcher performance).

Called Strike Probability

Called Strike Probability (CSP) is a number that represents the likelihood that all of a pitcher's pitches will be called a strike while controlling for location, pitcher and batter handedness, umpire and count. Here's how it works: on each pitch, our model determines how many times (out of 100) that a similar pitch was called for a strike given those factors mentioned above, and when normalized for each batter's strike zone. Then we average the CSP for all pitches thrown by a pitcher in a season, and that gives us the yearly CSP percentage you see in the stats boxes.

As you might imagine, pitchers with a higher CSP are more likely to work in the zone, where pitchers with a lower CSP are likely locating their pitches outside the normal strike zone, for better or for worse.

Projections

Many of you aren't turning to this book just for a look at what a player has done, but for a look at what a player is going to do: the PECOTA projections. PECOTA, initially developed by Nate Silver (who has moved on to greater fame as a political analyst), consists of three parts:

1. Major-league equivalencies, which use minor-league statistics to project how a player will perform in the major leagues;
2. Baseline forecasts, which use weighted averages and regression to the mean to estimate a player's current true talent level; and
3. Aging curves, which uses the career paths of comparable players to estimate how a player's statistics are likely to change over time.

With all those important things covered, let's take a look at what's in the book this year.

Team Prospectus

Most of this book is composed of team chapters, with one for each of the 30 major-league franchises. On the first page of each chapter, you'll see a box that contains some of the key statistics for each team as well as a very inviting stadium diagram. (You can see an example of this for the Milwaukee Brewers on this very page!)

We start with the team name, their unadjusted 2019 win-loss record, and their divisional ranking. Beneath that are a host of other team statistics. **Pythag** presents an adjusted 2019 winning percentage, calculated by taking runs scored per game (**RS/G**) and runs allowed per game (**RA/G**) for the team, and running them through a version of Bill James' Pythagorean formula that was refined and improved by David Smyth and Brandon Heipp. (The formula is called "Pythagenpat," which is equally fun to type and to say.)

Next up is **DRC+**, described earlier, to indicate the overall hitting ability of the team either above or below league-average. Run prevention on the pitching side is covered by **DRA** (also mentioned earlier) and another metric: Fielding Independent Pitching (**FIP**), which calculates another ERA-like statistic based on strikeouts, walks, and home runs recorded. Defensive Efficiency Rating (**DER**) tells us the percentage of balls in play turned into outs for the team, and is a quick fielding shorthand that rounds out run prevention.

After that, we have several measures related to roster composition, as opposed to on-field performance. **B-Age** and **P-Age** tell us the average age of a team's batters and pitchers, respectively. **Salary** is the combined team payroll for all on-field players, and Doug Pappas' Marginal Dollars per Marginal Win (**M$/MW**) tells us how much money a team spent to earn production above replacement level.

Ending this batch of statistics is the number of disabled list days a team had over the season (**IL Days**) and the amount of salary paid to players on the disabled list (**$ on IL**); this final number is expressed as a percentage of total payroll.

Next to each of these stats, we've listed each team's MLB rank in that category from first to 30th. In this, first always indicates a positive outcome and 30th a negative outcome, except in the case of salary—first is highest.

After the franchise statistics, we share a few items about the team's home ballpark. There's the aforementioned diagram of the park's dimensions (including distances to the outfield wall), a graphic showing the height of the wall from the left-field pole to the right-field pole, and a table showing three-year park factors for the stadium. The park factors are displayed as indexes where 100 is average, 110 means that the park inflates the statistic in question by 10 percent, and 90 means that the park deflates the statistic in question by 10 percent.

On the second page of each team chapter, you'll find three graphs. The first is the **2019 Hit List Ranking**. This shows our Hit List Rank for the team on each day of the 2019 season and is intended to give you a picture of the ups and downs of the team's season. Hit List Rank measures overall team performance and drives the Hit List Power Rankings at the baseballprospectus.com website.

The second graph is **Committed Payroll** and helps you see how the team's payroll has compared to the MLB and divisional average payrolls over time. Payroll figures are current as of January 1, 2020; with so many free agents still unsigned as of this writing, the final 2020 figure will likely be significantly different for many teams. (In the meantime, you can always find the most current data at Baseball Prospectus' Cot's Baseball Contracts page.)

The third graph is **Farm System Ranking** and displays how the Baseball Prospectus prospect team has ranked the organization's farm system since 2007.

After the graphs, we have a **Personnel** section that lists many of the important decision-makers and upper-level field and operations staff members for the franchise, as well as any former Baseball Prospectus staff members who are currently part of the organization. (In very rare circumstances, someone might be on both lists!)

Juan Soto LF

Born: 10/25/98 Age: 21 Bats: L Throws: L
Height: 6'1" Weight: 185 Origin: International Free Agent, 2015

YEAR	TEAM	LVL	AGE	PA	R	2B	3B	HR	RBI	BB	K	SB	CS	AVG/OBP/SLG
2017	NAT	RK	18	27	3	1	1	0	4	2	1	0	0	.320/.370/.440
2017	HAG	A	18	96	15	5	0	3	14	10	8	1	2	.360/.427/.523
2018	HAG	A	19	74	12	5	3	5	24	14	13	2	0	.373/.486/.814
2018	POT	A+	19	73	17	3	1	7	18	11	8	0	1	.371/.466/.790
2018	HAR	AA	19	35	4	2	0	2	10	4	7	1	0	.323/.400/.581
2018	WAS	MLB	19	494	77	25	1	22	70	79	99	5	2	.292/.406/.517
2019	WAS	MLB	20	659	110	32	5	34	110	108	132	12	1	.282/.401/.548
2020	WAS	MLB	21	630	92	30	3	35	102	85	123	5	2	.284/.382/.543

Comparables: Ronald Acuña Jr., Mike Trout, Tony Conigliaro

YEAR	TEAM	LVL	AGE	PA	DRC+	VORP	BABIP	BRR	FRAA	WARP
2017	NAT	RK	18	27	135	1.5	.333	0.0	RF(9): -1.1	0.0
2017	HAG	A	18	96	181	8.0	.373	1.0	RF(19): -1.9, LF(2): -0.3	0.9
2018	HAG	A	19	74	222	14.5	.405	0.3	RF(14): 1.1, CF(2): 0.2	1.2
2018	POT	A+	19	73	260	15.4	.340	1.4	RF(14): 1.0, LF(1): 0.0	1.6
2018	HAR	AA	19	35	113	3.6	.364	0.0	LF(4): 0.6, RF(4): -0.5	0.1
2018	WAS	MLB	19	494	125	40.5	.338	-0.5	LF(114): 2.7	3.0
2019	WAS	MLB	20	659	136	49.0	.312	1.4	LF(150): -0.8	4.9
2020	WAS	MLB	21	630	133	43.6	.310	-0.1	LF 3	4.8

Position Players

After all that information and a thoughtful bylined essay covering each team, we present our player comments. These are also bylined, but due to frequent franchise shifts during the offseason, our bylines are more a rough guide than a perfect accounting of who wrote what.

Each player is listed with the major-league team that employed him as of early January 2020. If a player changed teams after that point via free agency, trade, or any other method, you'll be able to find them in the chapter for their previous squad.

As an example, take a look at the player comment for Nationals outfielder Juan Soto: the stat block that accompanies his written comment is at the top of this page. First we cover biographical information (age is as of June 30, 2020) before moving onto the stats themselves. Our statistic columns include standard identifying information like **YEAR**, **TEAM**, **LVL** (level of affiliated play) and **AGE** before getting into the numbers. Next, we provide raw, untranslated numbers like you might find on the back of your dad's baseball cards: **PA** (plate appearances), **R** (runs), **2B** (doubles), **3B** (triples), **HR** (home runs), **RBI** (runs batted in), **BB** (walks), **K** (strikeouts), **SB** (stolen bases) and **CS** (caught stealing).

Next, we have unadjusted "slash" statistics: **AVG** (batting average), **OBP** (on-base percentage) and **SLG** (slugging percentage). Following the slash line is **DRC+** (Deserved Runs Created Plus), which we described earlier as total offensive expected contribution compared to the league average.

One of our oldest active metrics, **VORP** (Value Over Replacement Player), considers offensive production, position and plate appearances. In essence, it is the number of runs contributed beyond what a replacement-level player at the same position would contribute if given the same percentage of team plate appearances. VORP does not consider the quality of a player's defense.

BABIP (batting average on balls in play) tells us how often a ball in play fell for a hit, and can help us identify whether a batter may have been lucky or not...but note that high BABIPs also tend to follow the great hitters of our time, as well as speedy singles hitters who put the ball on the ground.

The next item is **BRR** (Baserunning Runs), which covers all of a player's baserunning accomplishments including (but not limited to) swiped bags and failed attempts. Next is **FRAA** (Fielding Runs Above Average), which also includes the number of games previously played at each position noted in parentheses. Multi-position players have only their two most frequent positions listed here, but their total FRAA number reflects all positions played.

Our last column here is **WARP** (Wins Above Replacement Player). WARP estimates the total value of a player, which means for hitters it takes into account hitting runs above average (calculated using the DRC+ model), BRR and FRAA. Then, it makes an adjustment for positions played and gives the player a credit for plate appearances based upon the difference between "replacement level"—which is derived from the quality of players added to a team's roster after the start of the season–and the league average.

The final line just below the stats box is **PECOTA** data, which is discussed further in a following section.

Catchers

Catchers are a special breed, and thus they have earned their own separate box which displays some of the defensive metrics that we've built just for them. As an example, let's check out J.T. Realmuto.

The **YEAR** and **TEAM** columns match what you'd find in the other stat box. **P. COUNT** indicates the number of pitches thrown while the catcher was behind the plate, including swinging strikes, fouls and balls in play. **FRM RUNS** is the total run value the catcher provided (or cost) his team by influencing the umpire to call strikes where other catchers did not. **BLK RUNS** expresses the total run value above or below average for the catcher's ability to prevent wild pitches and passed balls. **THRW RUNS** is calculated using a similar model as the previous two statistics, and it measures a catcher's ability to throw out basestealers but also to dissuade them from testing his arm in the first place. It takes into account factors like the pitcher (including his delivery and pickoff move) and baserunner (who could be as fast as Billy Hamilton or as slow as Yonder Alonso). **TOT RUNS** is the sum of all of the previous three statistics.

Justin Verlander RHP
Born: 02/20/83   Age: 37   Bats: R   Throws: R
Height: 6'5"   Weight: 225   Origin: Round 1, 2004 Draft (#2 overall)

YEAR	TEAM	LVL	AGE	W	L	SV	G	GS	IP	H	HR	BB/9	K/9	K	GB%	BABIP
2017	DET	MLB	34	10	8	0	28	28	172	153	23	3.5	9.2	176	34%	.283
2017	HOU	MLB	34	5	0	0	5	5	34	17	4	1.3	11.4	43	32%	.194
2018	HOU	MLB	35	16	9	0	34	34	214	156	28	1.6	12.2	290	31%	.272
2019	HOU	MLB	36	21	6	0	34	34	223	137	36	1.7	12.1	300	36%	.219
2020	HOU	MLB	37	15	6	0	29	29	184	138	28	2.3	12.1	248	35%	.274

Comparables: Zack Greinke, A.J. Burnett, Aníbal Sánchez

YEAR	TEAM	LVL	AGE	WHIP	ERA	DRA	WARP	MPH	FB%	WHF	CSP
2017	DET	MLB	34	1.28	3.82	4.03	3.0	97.7	58	11	47.8
2017	HOU	MLB	34	0.65	1.06	3.08	0.9	97.5	59.6	15.1	49.9
2018	HOU	MLB	35	0.90	2.52	2.33	7.3	97.5	61.2	16.2	51.6
2019	HOU	MLB	36	0.80	2.58	2.51	7.9	96.8	49.9	17.5	48.3
2020	HOU	MLB	37	1.01	2.75	2.95	5.3	95.8	54.6	15.1	48.2

Pitchers

Let's give our pitchers a turn, using 2019 AL Cy Young winner Justin Verlander as our example. Take a look at his stat block: the first line and the **YEAR**, **TEAM**, **LVL** and **AGE** columns are the same as in the position player example earlier.

Here too, we have a series of columns that display raw, unadjusted statistics compiled by the pitcher over the course of a season: **W** (wins), **L** (losses), **SV** (saves), **G** (games pitched), **GS** (games started), **IP** (innings pitched), **H** (hits allowed) and **HR** (home runs allowed). Next we have two statistics that are rates: **BB/9** (walks per nine innings) and **K/9** (strikeouts per nine innings), before returning to the unadjusted K (strikeouts).

Next up is **GB%** (ground ball percentage), which is the percentage of all batted balls that were hit on the ground, including both outs and hits. Remember, this is based on observational data and subject to human error, so please approach this with a healthy dose of skepticism.

BABIP (batting average on balls in play) is calculated using the same methodology as it is for position players, but it often tells us more about a pitcher than it does a hitter. With pitchers, a high BABIP is often due to poor defense or bad luck, and can often be an indicator of potential rebound, and a low BABIP may be cause to expect performance regression. (A typical league-average BABIP is close to .290-.300.)

The metrics **WHIP** (walks plus hits per inning pitched) and **ERA** (earned run average) are old standbys: WHIP measures walks and hits allowed on a per-inning basis, while ERA measures earned runs on a nine-inning basis. Neither of these stats are translated or adjusted.

DRA (Deserved Run Average) was described at length earlier, and measures how many runs the pitcher "deserved" to allow per nine innings. Please note that since we lack all the data points that would make for a "real" DRA for minor-league events, the DRA displayed for minor league partial-seasons is based off of different data. (That data is a modified version of our cFIP metric, which you can find more information about on our website.)

Just like with hitters, **WARP** (Wins Above Replacement Player) is a total value metric that puts pitchers of all stripes on the same scale as position players. We use DRA as the primary input for our calculation of WARP. You might notice that relief pitchers (due to their limited innings) may have a lower WARP than you were expecting or than you might see in other WARP-like metrics. WARP does not take leverage into account, just the actions a pitcher performs and the expected value of those actions...which ends up judging high-leverage relief pitchers differently than you might imagine given their prestige and market value.

MPH gives you the pitcher's 95th percentile velocity for the noted season, in order to give you an idea of what the *peak* fastball velocity a pitcher possesses. Since this comes from our pitch-tracking data, it is not publicly available for minor-league pitchers.

Finally, we display the three new pitching metrics we described earlier. **FB%** (fastball percentage) gives you the percentage of fastballs thrown out of all pitches. **WHF** (whiff rate) tells you the percentage of swinging strikes induced out of all pitches. **CSP** (called strike probability) expresses the likelihood of all pitches thrown to result in a called strike, after controlling for factors like handedness, umpire, pitch type, count and location.

PECOTA

All players have PECOTA projections for 2020, as well as a set of other numbers that describe the performance of comparable players according to PECOTA. All projections for 2020 are for the player at the date we went to press in early January and are projected into the league and park context as indicated by the team abbreviation. (Note that players at very low levels of the minors are too unpredictable to assess using these numbers.) All PECOTA projected statistics represent a player's projected major-league performance.

Below the projections are the player's three highest-scoring comparable players as determined by PECOTA. All comparables represent a snapshot of how the listed player was performing at the same age as the current player, so if a

23-year-old pitcher is compared to Bartolo Colón, he's actually being compared to a 23-year-old Colón, not the version that pitched for the Rangers in 2018, nor to Colón's career as a whole.

A few points about pitcher projections. First, we aren't yet projecting peak velocity, so that column will be blank in the PECOTA lines. Second, projecting DRA is trickier than evaluating past performance, because it is unclear how deserving each pitcher will be of his anticipated outcomes. However, we know that another DRA-related statistic–contextual FIP or cFIP–estimates future run scoring very well. So for PECOTA, the projected DRA figures you see are based on the past cFIPs generated by the pitcher and comparable players over time, along with the other factors described above.

Lineouts

In each chapter's Lineouts section, you'll find abbreviated text comments, as well as all the same information you'd find in our full player comments. The only difference is that we limit the stats boxes in this section to only including the 2019 information for each player.

Managers

After all those wonderful team chapters, we've got statistics for each big-league manager, all of whom are organized by alphabetical order. Here you'll find a block including an extraordinary amount of information collected from each manager's entire career. For more information on the acronyms and what they mean, please visit the Glossary at www.baseballprospectus.com.

There is one important metric that we'd like to call attention to, and you'll find it next to each manager's name: **wRM+** (weighted reliever management plus). Developed by Rob Arthur and Rian Watt, wRM+ investigates how good a manager is at using their best relievers during the moments of highest leverage, using both our proprietary DRA metric as well as Leverage Index. wRM+ is scaled to a league average of 100, and a wRM+ of 105 indicates that relievers were used approximately five percent "better" than average. On the other hand, a wRM+ of 95 would tell us the team used its relievers five percent "worse" than the average team.

While wRM+ does not have an extremely strong correlation with a manager, it is statistically significant; this means that a manager is not *entirely* responsible for a team's wRM+, but does have some effect on that number.

PECOTA Leaderboards

If you're familiar with PECOTA, then you'll have noticed that the projection system often appears bullish on players coming off a bad year and bearish on players coming off a good year. (This is because the system weights several previous seasons, not just the most recent one.) In addition, we publish the 50th

Washington Nationals 2020

percentile projections for each player–which is smack in the middle of the range of projected production—which tends to mean PECOTA stat lines don't often have extreme results like 40 home runs or 250 strikeouts in a given season. In essence, PECOTA doesn't project very many extreme seasons.

At the end of the book, we've ranked the top players at each position based on their PECOTA projections. This might help you visualize just how a given player's projection compares to that of their peers, so that even if a dramatic stat line isn't projected, you can still imagine how they stack up against the rest of the league.

Part 1: Team Analysis

Washington Nationals: Where Are You Going, Where Have You Been?

Jarrett Seidler, Scott Delp and Matthew Trueblood

2019: What Went Right

The Nationals went on one of the greatest magic carpet rides in baseball history. They started at a glacial pace, bottoming out at 12 games below .500 before they even hit Memorial Day. They were one of the best teams in baseball from that point forward, but it was only enough to get them to the Wild Card Game. Down 3-1 in the eighth inning, they rallied late against NL Reliever of the Year Josh Hader. They were down 3-1 again in the eighth in Game 5 of the NLDS and won in extras. They fell behind early facing elimination in World Series Games 6 and 7 and rallied in both.

As for the banalities of the regular season, a lot of Washington's stars performed at or in excess of projections. Anthony Rendon was a leading MVP candidate. Juan Soto basically xeroxed his historic rookie season and is one of the best hitters through his age-20 season in baseball history. Victor Robles developed into one of the premiere defensive players in the game and continued to show promise at the plate. Max Scherzer, Stephen Strasburg, and Patrick Corbin provided more than 580 innings of ace starting pitching. Older veteran options like Howie Kendrick, Aníbal Sánchez, and Kurt Suzuki chipped in much more value than could have reasonably been expected. All would go on to star in the postseason.

For the most part, the Nats had good health and good performances. They were second in the National League in runs scored and third in DRC+. They were second in all of baseball in starting pitcher DRA. When you win 93 games, things have generally gone pretty well. They got hot at the best time you can get hot, but it's not that hard to see why this team rolled in the playoffs and won the World Series: They were genuinely a top-tier team all along, with but one big exception.

2019: What Went Wrong

The Nationals might've had the worst regular-season bullpen performance not just in the majors in 2019, but in modern memory. Their bullpen ERA was 5.68, which is atrocious, but also somehow substantially undersells how much the bullpen hurt the team in terms of actual wins and losses. They became the first team this century to be more than 10 wins below average by relief WPA (per FanGraphs). Their most effective reliever was by DRA was Tanner Rainey, who walked more than seven batters per nine.

They did make a few key upgrades along the way that proved to be important in the playoffs. Before the deadline, they traded for Daniel Hudson. He fell into the closer's role by default in late-September and pitched well down the stretch and in the postseason. Hudson isn't an elite reliever, but he's decent enough that it's strange that he keeps being discarded every spring. They also got a usable half-season out of the ageless Fernando Rodney after he was released in Oakland. It was still a flaming dumpster overall, but they shortened the staff in the playoffs and were able to leverage the decent dudes like Hudson and Sean Doolittle alongside running starters on their throw days.

Despite the bullpen—and this is quite a testament to the quality of the rest of the team—the Nats only finished four games out in the NL East. They'd have won the division with even a bad bullpen, but this was something substantially beyond that. Those extra losses from the bullpen sent them on the toughest possible road through the playoffs: first through the Wild Card Game itself, where they burned both Scherzer and Strasburg to squeak past Milwaukee, then to a first-round matchup against the Dodgers. In the end, this all just made the journey to victory that much better. *—Jarrett Seidler*

Prospect Outlook

The Nats navigated 2019 with almost no help from their farm. It's a thin system with quality at the very top in shortstop **Carter Kieboom** and **Luis Garcia**, but there is a good bit of uncertainty after that. Kieboom did everything expected of him at Triple-A, though he may need a swing adjustment to get to the game power he's capable of having. He'll be somewhere in the Washington infield next season, likely at either second or third base—Starlin Castro and Asdrúbal Cabrera are placeholders at best.

Garcia won't turn 20 until May and is still another season or two away, especially after struggling a bit in Double-A this season. He is aggressive and makes enough contact, but likely needs to improve his selectivity to get to more of his hit tool. That might also help him figure out which pitches he can turn on and drive as he took more of a defensive, all-field approach in Harrisburg.

Most of the remainder of the Washington top prospects is made up of arms taken in the last few drafts, led by 2019 first rounder **Jackson Rutledge**. The 6-foot-8 Rutledge has a solid repertoire, but also the command questions you might expect from a pitcher of that size. His pro debut was encouraging, finishing with 27 1/3 innings in full-season A-ball, but he has a long road ahead. **Tim Cate** and **Mason Denaburg** are two 2018 draftees who had vastly different seasons in 2019, with Denaburg pitching just 20 1/3 innings due to shoulder issues. Cate found his way to High-A with good success, riding an average fastball and above-average curve. **Wil Crowe** stayed healthy in 2019 and that was a big step forward for him. He is the closest to being ready to help the big club of all the arms mentioned here and he has everything he needs from a stuff standpoint to be a useful back-end starter. Crowe did struggle somewhat in a promotion to Triple-A and that was likely just as much a function of workload as anything. A rested Crowe should be able to start back in the PCL in 2020 and be ready to contribute in DC by midseason.

On the hitting side, first baseman **Drew Mendoza** and outfielder **Gage Canning** are names from recent draft classes who each have some upside. Infielder **Yasel Antuna** was signed in the same international free agent class as Garcia, and he was considered at the time to be the more intriguing prospect, but he missed almost all of 2019 with elbow trouble. The rest of the system is largely a collection of questionable arms and young IFA signings that can't be expected to provide any impact help in the near future. That may not change a lot very soon as the team will likely have to make a few trades, as well as pull off some quality free agent signings, in order to keep their window of contention open for a couple more seasons. —*Scott Delp*

2020 Outlook

No World Series champion in recent memory has been so proactive. Re-signing Strasburg was a no-brainer, albeit one which required both Strasburg's cooperation and a lot of money. Still, Mike Rizzo deserves some praise just for getting that much done. Retaining Rendon would have been a wonderful bonus, but even in this era, in which we better understand how much teams make and in which we demand that they reinvest that revenue, it's hard to justify a pair of deals totaling nearly $500 million in guaranteed money.

Instead of keeping Rendon, and rather than ponying up (either in dollars or in prospects) for a high-profile replacement, Rizzo elected to put together an interwoven platoon across three infield positions. Starlin Castro and Eric Thames join the returning Kendrick, Ryan Zimmerman, and Asdrúbal Cabrera in a crowded set of non-shortstops, and Kieboom figures to hit his way back into the picture, too. This feels like an arrangement that wouldn't have worked with 25-man rosters, but it should be a viable one with 26 slots, especially because that particular collection of players is unlikely to be simultaneously healthy very often.

Washington Nationals 2020

Rizzo's commitment to staying strong across the infield was impressive, and he went almost as far in reinforcing the bullpen. Retaining Hudson as a complement to Doolittle was the obvious move but adding Will Harris to the mix should give the Nationals as good a three-man rotation through the final two innings of close games as any team in the NL. Rizzo also traded a player taken in the ninth round in June to get Ryne Harper in late January, a sneaky-good move that bolsters the team's depth without crowding the roster. (Harper can be optioned to the minor leagues.) While one can't understate the loss of Rendon, the Nats head into 2020 as well-rounded and nearly as talented as they were in October. —*Matthew Trueblood*

Performance Graphs

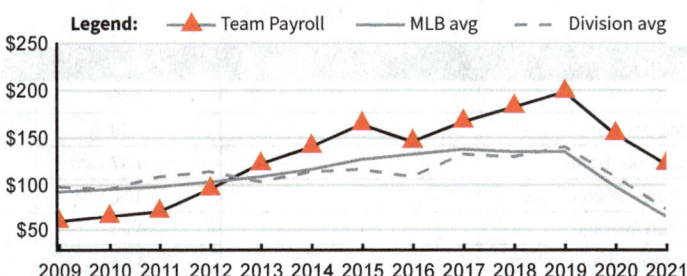

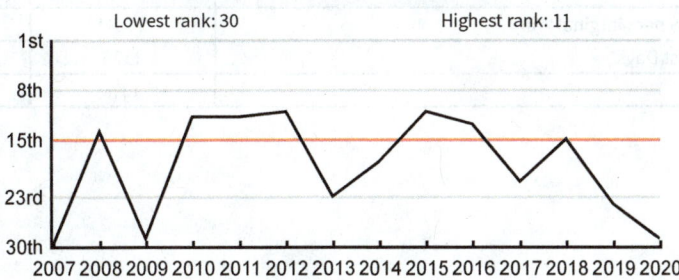

2019 Team Performance

ACTUAL STANDINGS

Team	W	L	Pct
ATL	97	65	0.599
WAS	**93**	**69**	**0.574**
NYN	86	76	0.531
PHI	81	81	0.500
MIA	57	105	0.352

THIRD-ORDER STANDINGS

Team	W	L	Pct
WAS	**95**	**67**	**0.584**
ATL	89	73	0.550
NYN	88	74	0.542
PHI	74	88	0.457
MIA	60	102	0.373

TOP HITTERS

Player	WARP
Anthony Rendon	6.3
Juan Soto	4.9
Trea Turner	4.0

TOP PITCHERS

Player	WARP
Stephen Strasburg	8.3
Max Scherzer	6.2
Patrick Corbin	5.9

VITAL STATISTICS

Statistic Name	Value	Rank
Pythagenpat	.589	6th
Runs Scored per Game	5.39	6th
Runs Allowed per Game	4.47	9th
Deserved Runs Created Plus	101	9th
Deserved Run Average	4.03	2nd
Fielding Independent Pitching	4.08	6th
Defensive Efficiency Rating	.704	15th
Batter Age	28.5	23rd
Pitcher Age	30.7	29th
Salary	$197.2M	4th
Marginal $ per Marginal Win	$4.1M	13th
Injured List Days	1126	17th
$ on IL	13%	10th

2020 Team Projections

PROJECTED STANDINGS

Team	W	L	Pct	+/-
NYN	87.8	74.2	0.542	2
WAS	**87.1**	**74.9**	**0.538**	**-6**
ATL	82.8	79.2	0.511	-14
PHI	76.8	85.2	0.474	-4
MIA	71.3	90.7	0.440	14

TOP PROJECTED HITTERS

Player	WARP
Juan Soto	4.7
Trea Turner	3.6
Victor Robles	2.7

TOP PROJECTED PITCHERS

Player	WARP
Max Scherzer	5.6
Stephen Strasburg	4.5
Patrick Corbin	3.6

FARM SYSTEM REPORT

Top Prospect	Number of Top 101 Prospects
Carter Kieboom, #11	1

KEY DEDUCTIONS

Player	WARP
Anthony Rendon	3.7
Brian Dozier	0.4
Matt Adams	0.0

KEY ADDITIONS

Player	WARP
Eric Thames	0.9
Will Harris	0.7
Starlin Castro	0.6
Ben Braymer	0.4
Ryne Harper	0.1
Wil Crowe	0.1
Kyle Finnegan	0.0
Welington Castillo	-0.1

Team Personnel

General Manager & President of Baseball Operations
Mike Rizzo

Assistant General Manager & Vice President, Player Personnel
Doug Harris

Assistant General Manager & Vice President, Scouting Operations
Kris Kline

Manager
Dave Martinez

Nationals Park Stats

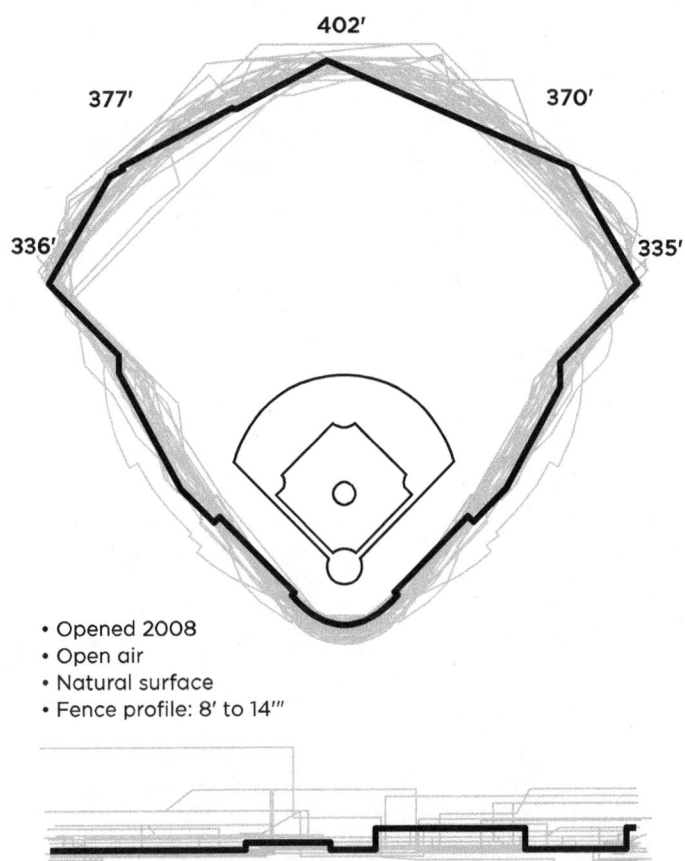

- Opened 2008
- Open air
- Natural surface
- Fence profile: 8' to 14'''

Three-Year Park Factors

Runs	Runs/RH	Runs/LH	HR/RH	HR/LH
104	104	105	108	107

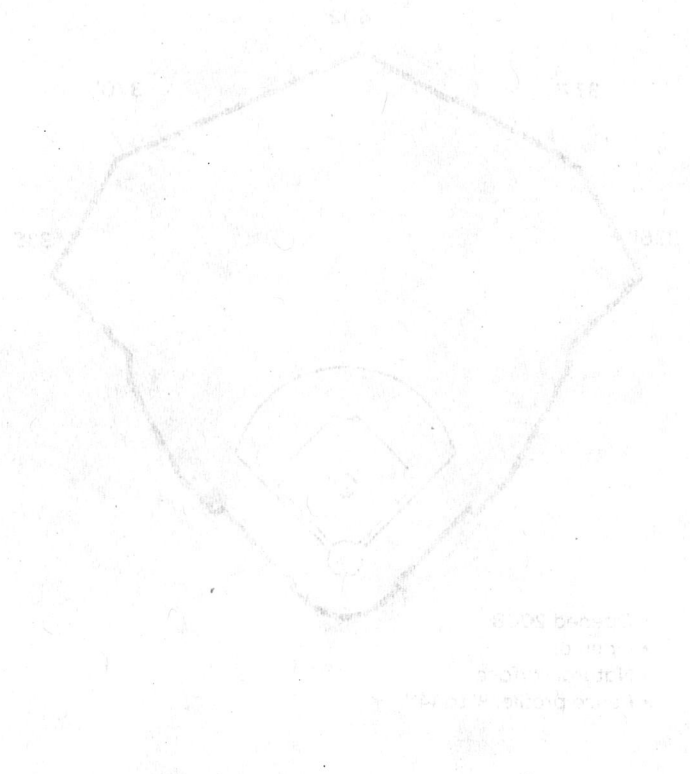

Nationals Team Analysis

Every year of my childhood just before the weather fully began to warm, I caught a mysterious, undiagnosable, 24-hour illness that absolutely demanded that I could not go to school or work. When I was in elementary school, my dad would pull me out of class in the morning. I was sick, you see. So sick. Very sick. I absolutely had to be taken to a sacred holy place that could cure me. It just so happened that the perfect remedy for my illness was the smell of freshly cut grass, and the rumble of a low-flying jet, and the taste of a hot dog. Weirdly, I always got very sick on the exact day when I could have all of these things: Opening Day.

My dad and I went together. We usually sat in the outfield, on flaming hot plastic seats, and we grinned. We nudged each other in the ribs and pointed: look at the new awnings; look at the old ladies with their scorebooks; look at our team. Every year, it was one of my best days. Every year there was the possibility that this could be The Year, our year. It vibrates in the air, the hope.

As an adult, I missed Opening Day. The city where I got my undergraduate degree didn't have a major league baseball team, and it never worked out for me to drive home. When I moved to Washington, D.C. after college, the season had already started, and I was miserable. It was summer. I had just started a new job that required me to work constantly. I was all alone in a big new city on a completely different coast and quickly acquired a healthy dose of culture shock. I had lived in Texas my entire life, and I was lonely. For the first time, I had coworkers, but I didn't have any friends. When I called home, I tried to play down how upset I was, how isolated, how even the light and the sky here looked different. When my dad updated me on the IL and the team's failures (they were always failing in new spectacular ways), I was jealous. I didn't get any of their games on my cable.

"You know," my dad said. "It wouldn't be so bad if you adopted the Nationals as your team." He had good reasons: I could learn about double-switches and the National League. I could watch all the games on TV. And plus, they were the home team. My dad himself grew up a Braves fan, and when he moved to Texas an adult, switched over to the Rangers.

So I began that summer to watch this new team who was all hyped up over their 10 year anniversary. It is hard to adjust to a new team, even one as newly minted as the Washington Nationals. There is a whole culture to adapt to; a history of inside jokes and truly inside baseball. So much of watching a baseball game is knowing the small things. Understanding which players have long-held grudges and which ones are hometown heroes takes time. And it was frustrating. Here I was with a team I didn't know anything about, in a city I hadn't learned yet how to love. On my birthday that year, as a special gift to me, the Washington Nationals played a franchise record breaking 5 hour and 34 minute game against the Dodgers, not yet a personal enemy, and won.

I had moved to Washington, D.C. blindly. I had a job offer and accepted it sight unseen. Whenever I told people I was moving here, to the capital city of our country, most wrinkled their noses. Why, my friends and family back home asked, would you want to live on the east coast? Why, my friends who had moved to New York asked, would you want to live in a city that only cares about politics? I quickly learned all the derogatory jokes made at the city's expense. A D.C. 8, people snickered, was a Los Angeles 3. Everyone wore suits from Brooks Brothers. No one, they said, stays there. If you outlive one administration, these people said, you can call yourself a native.

Almost six years later, I know that all of this is an ugly stereotype created by people who never had any intention of staying. Those people, I know now, are the ones who wear their childhood team's jerseys to the games, the ones who never bother to learn what this city really is. It is easy to believe them. Watching the broadcast, even, of this year's World Series games, the only parts of Washington, D.C. that got shown were the monuments and the White House and the Capitol. And while those are iconic landmarks that I, too, love to visit, they aren't the city. That is the federal district.

The city itself is as diverse and interesting and varied as any other metropolitan American city. There are independent bookstores and art galleries and Michelin-starred restaurants. There are bars near the Capitol with drink specials that accompany the C-SPAN showing of the impeachment trials and there are the bars I go to with sticky counters and a team wearing red (always red) playing on televisions. Washington, D.C. is home to both Georgetown University and Howard University. There are public schools and bus routes and almost 700,000 people who live and work here. In the spring, all of the trees bloom pink at once. It is the kind of city that makes a smart joke about its biggest issue on the license plates. They read at the bottom: "Taxation Without Representation."

At the third game of the World Series, activists stood on Half Street between still-forming condos, and handed out red flyers with the outline of the district on them. These were to advocate for D.C. statehood, something 79 percent of the residents of the city voted for in a 2016 ballot. Like Puerto Rico, the people who live in D.C. do not have any voting representation in Congress. United States citizens are entitled to representation in both the House and the Senate, and yet for decades the federal government has refused to acknowledge that living right under their noses are 700,000 people, more people than both Vermont and Wyoming, without that constitutional right. (Puerto Rico has a higher population than 20 states.)

The narrative that no one lives in D.C. for more than two years is intentional and perpetuated with purpose. That statement erases the people of color who have lived in Washington, D.C. for generations through one of the highest murder rates in America, a heroin epidemic, a basketball team named the Bullets, and a football team named something worse. Almost 50 percent of the population of D.C. is black. Residents of D.C., like Puerto Rico, have been denied their rights to vote via that erasure. When new transplants say that "no one lives in D.C. for long," they're only showing their own bias. No one *they know* stays for long. But plenty of people stay, and a lot of them call this place home. And when a place is your home, when you live there really, you root for its teams. You wear red.

I haven't been in D.C. for anywhere near as long as a lot of other Nationals fans. I sat next to an older gentleman down the first-base line at an August game who told me about the first game in the new stadium in 2008, about how he, then in his 60s, had cried real tears. He had waited for most of his life for Washington, D.C. to have a baseball team again. He'd been forced to grow up without a team to root for, and here they were, finally, back again just for him.

I learned to love D.C. because the Washington Nationals were easy to love. They gave me more first round of the playoffs flops to bemoan with my neighbors than anyone could have wanted. They gave me perfect games. They gave me racing presidents. They gave me a wunderkind outfielder with hair like Johnny Bravo, and then one who still had his round teenage face. The arms of the Washington Nationals were always open to me, and where they at first provided me freedom from my loneliness, they soon provided me with community.

That is the beauty of a team, any team. Investing in a sport emotionally gives us something to love that we don't have to do anything at all for. Turning on the game on our smartphones at our desks remind us that we're more than the job we get a paycheck for. Leaning over the bar to check the score reminds us that we're part of a bigger community than just the one that we've chosen for ourselves. At their best, sports teams remind us that it is okay to care about something with childlike enthusiasm even when we have absolutely no reason to. Sports, we often forget, are supposed to be fun. The investment in a team just for fun, not for any kind of gain, is what binds a community together, what causes strangers to tip a cap at another curly W on the street, or (in October) to raise a hand to high-five.

The 2019 Washington Nationals were something special. Despite a truly awful May, they refused to crumble into a sinkhole and never recover. I don't know what happened in that locker room over Memorial Day weekend, but whatever it was worked. The team figured out how to play baseball, but they also seemed to remember suddenly that this thing they were doing is a game. That it is supposed to be fun. Gerrardo Parra changed his walkup song for his daughter and suddenly the entire stadium was clapping along to "Baby Shark." Max Scherzer bunted a ball *into his own face* at practice and went out and pitched anyway with two black eyes, and his teammates made fun of him! They sang "Calma." They were, from June 1st on, a joy to watch.

But the most beautiful thing about this 2019 Washington Nationals team was watching them give that community to one another. When Daniel Hudson chose to support his wife through the birth of his child instead of pitching Game 1 of the NLCS, Sean Doolittle faced the press and reprimanded those who criticized him. When Scherzer's back cramped so badly he couldn't dress himself, every single one of his teammates gave statements about how impressed they were with him, how they knew he wouldn't sit if he didn't absolutely have to. They hugged Stephen Strasburg. They danced in the dugout. They snapped little baby sharks at each other from second base when they hit doubles, and whatever it is Brian Dozier is doing with his shirt off in the locker room seems to be shadily supported by them all.

This year, I begged my friends to go to Opening Day with me, but they all had to work, and were not able to be sick like me. As the day approached, I grew sadder and sadder. I hadn't been to Opening Day in ten years. It felt unjust, insane, heretical. So at the encouragement of a friend, I bought a ticket to go alone. I brought my scorebook and wore my hat, and showed up to Opening Day with a chest full of hope. That's a thing people don't tell you about Washington, D.C.: it has so much hope. Here is a city that is filled with people who voted for statehood recognition despite every barrier set in front of them. Here are some people who moved from another state to work on a campaign or in a congressional office or for an NGO because they believe that maybe, just maybe, the world can change. Here is a fanbase that despite never managing to get past the first round of the playoffs showed up on a chilly day in late March with Bryce Harper's name crossed out on their jerseys to say to one another quietly "This may be our year. This could finally be it."

When you go to a game alone, you remember how much of watching a sport is joining a community. It is human nature, even when alone, to turn to the person next to you with wide eyes when Trea Turner stretches his body out like a cat to snatch a ball out of the air. It is natural, to turn around to give high-fives when Juan Soto rockets a ball over the outfield fence. It is required that on the first day of the season, you ask the stranger next to you what he thinks the team's chances are and nod your head yes when he says, "Absolutely this is it, this will be our year," even if you don't know if he's right.

The 2019 Washington Nationals lost their first game of the season to the New York Mets 0-2. "It was a pleasure sitting next to you," my neighbor said to me when the game ended. "This may not be our year after all." For him and for myself and for all of Washington, D.C., I'm so glad he was wrong.

—*Kelsey McKinney is a freelance reporter and former staff writer at Deadspin.*

Part 2: Player Analysis

PLAYER COMMENTS WITH GRAPHS

Asdrúbal Cabrera INF
Born: 11/13/85   Age: 34   Bats: B   Throws: R
Height: 6'0"   Weight: 205   Origin: International Free Agent, 2002

YEAR	TEAM	LVL	AGE	PA	R	2B	3B	HR	RBI	BB	K	SB	CS	AVG/OBP/SLG
2017	NYN	MLB	31	540	66	32	0	14	59	50	83	3	2	.280/.351/.434
2018	NYN	MLB	32	407	48	23	1	18	58	29	81	0	0	.277/.329/.488
2018	PHI	MLB	32	185	20	13	0	5	17	12	38	0	0	.228/.286/.392
2019	WAS	MLB	33	146	24	10	1	6	40	19	18	0	0	.323/.404/.565
2019	TEX	MLB	33	368	45	15	0	12	51	38	85	4	0	.235/.318/.393
2020	WAS	MLB	34	294	35	17	1	12	40	26	62	2	1	.268/.339/.468

Comparables: Cliff Pennington, Ian Kinsler, Delino DeShields

For an example of how little moves can pay off in unexpected ways, consider that the Nationals signed Cabrera in August following his release from the Rangers. Whereas he hadn't performed particularly well with Texas, instead looking like a 30-something-year-old infielder on his last legs, he dazzled with the Nationals during his second tour of duty in D.C. Cabrera hit, hit and hit some more, supplanting Brian Dozier on the depth chart by the time the postseason rolled around. He then drove in three runs in the World Series, a seven-game set in which the two teams were separated by—you guessed it—three runs. (The Astros actually outscored the Nationals by three runs, but never let facts interfere with vibes.) Every piece matters.

YEAR	TEAM	LVL	AGE	PA	DRC+	VORP	BABIP	BRR	FRAA	WARP
2017	NYN	MLB	31	540	104	30.7	.310	-2.2	SS(45): -0.2, 3B(44): -1.1	1.8
2018	NYN	MLB	32	407	105	29.3	.309	1.9	2B(90): -10.8	0.6
2018	PHI	MLB	32	185	107	4.3	.266	0.5	SS(31): -0.6, 3B(22): -0.5	0.8
2019	WAS	MLB	33	146	137	11.8	.330	-1.2	2B(31): -1.6, 3B(5): -0.3	0.9
2019	TEX	MLB	33	368	95	11.7	.278	0.2	3B(93): 6.0	1.8
2020	WAS	MLB	34	294	103	10.5	.311	-0.2	2B -3, 3B 0	0.9

Asdrúbal Cabrera, continued

Batted Ball Distribution

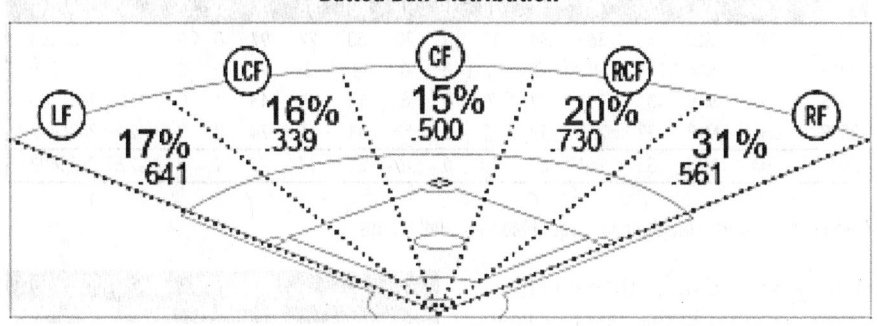

Strike Zone vs LHP   Strike Zone vs RHP

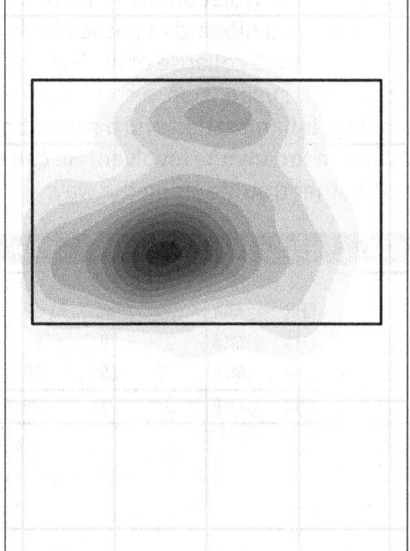

Washington Nationals 2020

Welington Castillo C

Born: 04/24/87   Age: 33   Bats: R   Throws: R
Height: 5'10"   Weight: 220   Origin: International Free Agent, 2004

YEAR	TEAM	LVL	AGE	PA	R	2B	3B	HR	RBI	BB	K	SB	CS	AVG/OBP/SLG
2017	BAL	MLB	30	365	44	11	0	20	53	22	97	0	0	.282/.323/.490
2018	CHR	AAA	31	40	2	1	0	0	3	3	11	0	0	.189/.250/.216
2018	CHA	MLB	31	181	17	7	0	6	15	9	46	1	0	.259/.304/.406
2019	CHA	MLB	32	251	19	12	0	12	41	16	74	0	0	.209/.267/.417
2020	CHA	MLB	33	251	27	10	0	10	32	17	75	1	0	.223/.282/.402

Comparables: Martín Maldonado, Miguel Montero, Jeff Mathis

Having secured more than half his career earnings in the past two years, Castillo probably won't look back on his time on the South Side entirely with disdain. Most everyone else will. And, since the worst offensive results of his career, a blizzard of passed balls

YEAR	TEAM	P. COUNT	FRM RUNS	BLK RUNS	THRW RUNS	TOT RUNS
2017	BAL	13481	6.8	1.3	3.2	12.4
2018	CHA	6226	-5.5	-0.8	0.1	-6.4
2019	CHA	6939	-10.5	-3.1	-0.3	-14.0
2020	CHA	14147	-7.5	-1.6	-0.8	-9.8

and a complete collapse of his framing performance were all scattered amid a bizarre PED suspension, a concussion, a pulled oblique that cost him a month, shoulder inflammation and a sore elbow (for good measure), it wasn't really a joyful run for anyone involved. He can still run into a dinger, but runs into too much other trouble along the way,

YEAR	TEAM	LVL	AGE	PA	DRC+	VORP	BABIP	BRR	FRAA	WARP
2017	BAL	MLB	30	365	114	21.0	.336	-0.7	C(88): 10.8	3.4
2018	CHR	AAA	31	40	60	-2.3	.269	-0.3	C(8): -0.5	-0.1
2018	CHA	MLB	31	181	93	4.6	.322	0.2	C(43): -6.5	0.0
2019	CHA	MLB	32	251	78	3.5	.247	-3.1	C(48): -13.7	-1.3
2020	CHA	MLB	33	251	79	0.4	.282	-0.8	C -10	-1.0

Welington Castillo, continued

Batted Ball Distribution

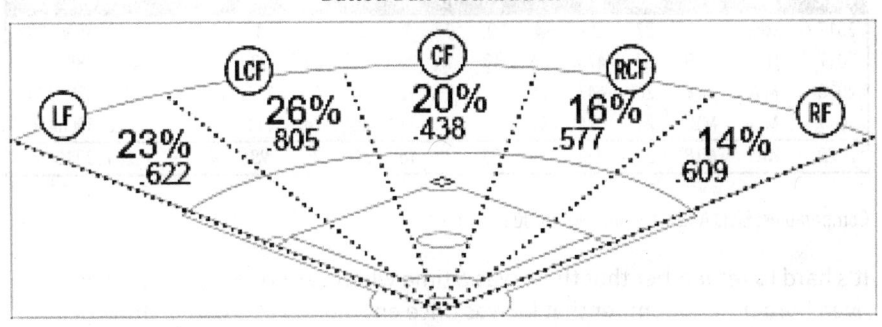

Strike Zone vs LHP   **Strike Zone vs RHP**

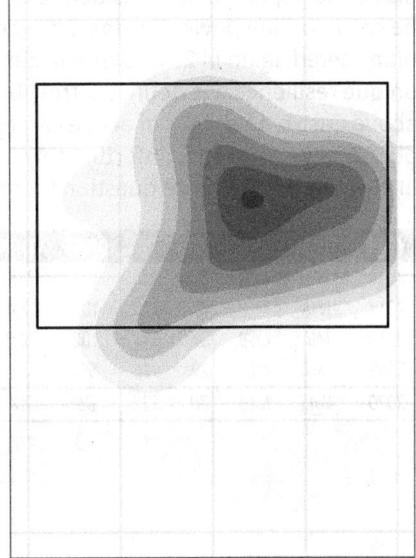

Nationals Player Analysis - 23

Starlin Castro   SS

Born: 03/24/90   Age: 30   Bats: R   Throws: R
Height: 6'2"   Weight: 230   Origin: International Free Agent, 2006

YEAR	TEAM	LVL	AGE	PA	R	2B	3B	HR	RBI	BB	K	SB	CS	AVG/OBP/SLG
2017	SWB	AAA	27	25	4	0	0	1	2	1	4	0	0	.333/.360/.458
2017	NYA	MLB	27	473	66	18	1	16	63	23	93	2	0	.300/.338/.454
2018	MIA	MLB	28	647	76	32	2	12	54	48	124	6	4	.278/.329/.400
2019	MIA	MLB	29	676	68	31	4	22	86	28	111	2	2	.270/.300/.436
2020	WAS	MLB	30	532	54	26	2	16	62	26	98	4	2	.264/.304/.416

Comparables: Elvis Andrus, Jean Segura, Juan Uribe

It's hard to remember that there was a time when Castro was a top prospect; it's even harder to remember that he was once envisioned as a cornerstone of a budding Cubs juggernaut (some things do change a lot in a decade, huh?). Ten years into his major league career, and Castro managed to turn in another season of slightly below-average offense, while taking a step back in the plate discipline department. Considering Castro's other faults—he's a poor defender, he has middling power, he doesn't hit for a high average anymore—his walk rate plummeted again in 2019, sapping almost any offensive value he had. Castro's unique resilience has defined a truly bizarre march to 1600 career hits: No player above Castro on the list of active career hits leaders is younger than he is, or has played fewer seasons. Unfortunately for him, that robust career hit total is more likely to become a trivia question that an entry in the record books.

YEAR	TEAM	LVL	AGE	PA	DRC+	VORP	BABIP	BRR	FRAA	WARP
2017	SWB	AAA	27	25	123	1.3	.368	0.4	2B(4): 0.1	0.2
2017	NYA	MLB	27	473	102	17.4	.347	0.5	2B(109): -4.9	1.1
2018	MIA	MLB	28	647	102	32.0	.330	0.3	2B(150): -6.2	1.6
2019	MIA	MLB	29	676	90	15.1	.293	-1.8	2B(117): -6.2, 3B(45): -0.3	0.6
2020	WAS	MLB	30	532	86	9.7	.301	-0.1	2B -5, 3B 0	0.5

Starlin Castro, continued

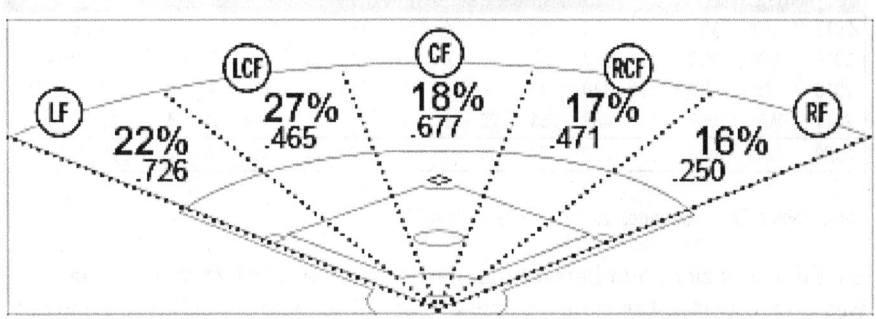

Batted Ball Distribution

| Strike Zone vs LHP | Strike Zone vs RHP |

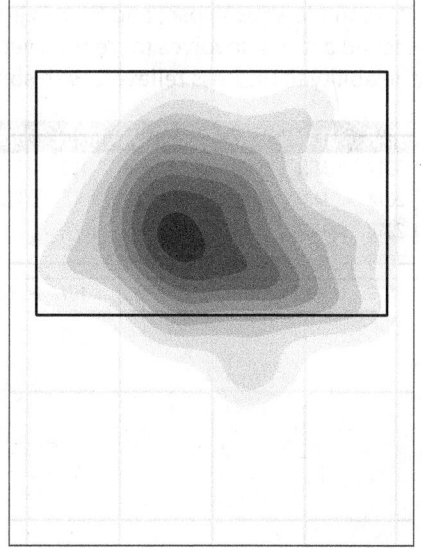

Brian Dozier 2B

Born: 05/15/87 Age: 33 Bats: R Throws: R
Height: 5'11" Weight: 200 Origin: Round 8, 2009 Draft (#252 overall)

YEAR	TEAM	LVL	AGE	PA	R	2B	3B	HR	RBI	BB	K	SB	CS	AVG/OBP/SLG
2017	MIN	MLB	30	705	106	30	4	34	93	78	141	16	7	.271/.359/.498
2018	MIN	MLB	31	462	65	21	2	16	52	46	96	8	3	.227/.307/.405
2018	LAN	MLB	31	170	16	9	0	5	20	24	33	4	0	.182/.300/.350
2019	WAS	MLB	32	482	54	20	0	20	50	61	105	3	4	.238/.340/.430
2020	WAS	MLB	33	350	44	14	1	16	47	41	80	7	2	.230/.327/.436

Comparables: Sean Rodríguez, Luis Valbuena, Kelly Johnson

Strip down Dozier's numbers for the season, and the bare fact remains that he was who he was last season: a below-average hitter with the ability to grind out at-bats by limiting his chases outside the zone. He's a dead pull hitter who—like so many of us—has only gotten entrenched in his ways as he's aged, as he's hit a total of one homer to the opposite field over the last two seasons. The history of second basemen entering their mid-30s looks a bit too much like the aftermath of a zombie apocalypse, and there's little in his profile that suggests Dozier has a second act that involves more than veteran leadership, professional at-bats and the ability to undress relievers with some late-inning power and pop.

YEAR	TEAM	LVL	AGE	PA	DRC+	VORP	BABIP	BRR	FRAA	WARP
2017	MIN	MLB	30	705	123	37.9	.300	2.2	2B(152): 9.7	5.4
2018	MIN	MLB	31	462	97	11.4	.256	1.6	2B(103): 1.9	1.6
2018	LAN	MLB	31	170	97	-1.6	.196	-1.6	2B(45): 0.1	0.3
2019	WAS	MLB	32	482	104	18.9	.271	-3.6	2B(123): -4.6, P(1): 0.0	1.0
2020	WAS	MLB	33	350	101	8.4	.260	-0.1	2B 0	1.2

Brian Dozier, continued

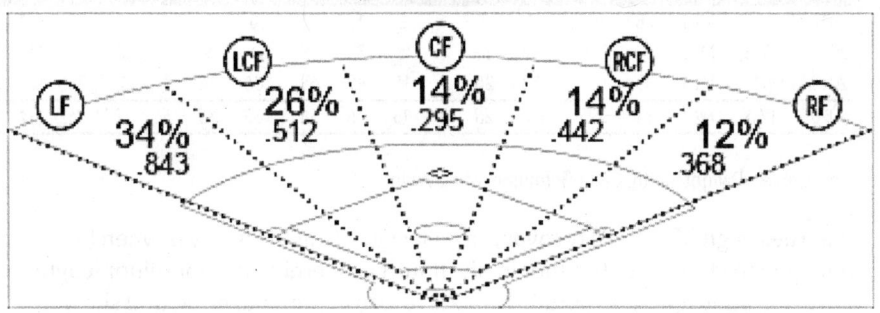

Batted Ball Distribution

Strike Zone vs LHP   Strike Zone vs RHP

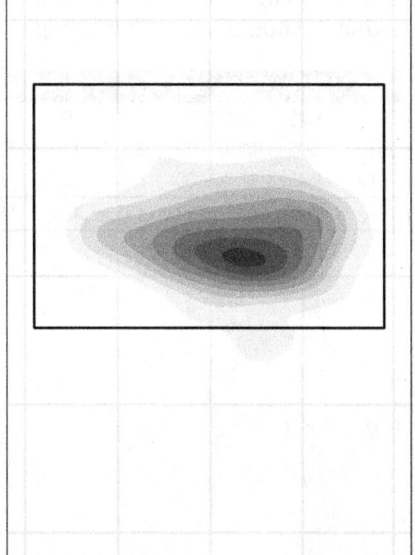

Washington Nationals 2020

Adam Eaton RF

Born: 12/06/88 Age: 31 Bats: L Throws: L
Height: 5'9" Weight: 176 Origin: Round 19, 2010 Draft (#571 overall)

YEAR	TEAM	LVL	AGE	PA	R	2B	3B	HR	RBI	BB	K	SB	CS	AVG/OBP/SLG
2017	WAS	MLB	28	107	24	7	1	2	13	14	18	3	1	.297/.393/.462
2018	WAS	MLB	29	370	55	18	1	5	33	38	64	9	1	.301/.394/.411
2019	WAS	MLB	30	656	103	25	7	15	49	65	106	15	3	.279/.365/.428
2020	WAS	MLB	31	595	68	28	5	15	68	58	103	13	5	.278/.362/.434

Comparables: Dwight Smith, Cesar Geronimo, Bruce Aven

The truest sign of Eaton's recovery from last year's ankle injury is when he managed to stick his entire foot in his mouth concerning pay for minor league players in June. Eaton eventually walked those comments back, and showed himself to be a serviceable outfielder and a consistent hitter, and a pest in the NLCS and World Series. But one can't help but compare Eaton with a former National wunderkind, just not the one you're probably thinking of; he's a bit of subtraction by addition in light of Lucas Giolito's All-Star season. Maybe the Nationals should have tried paying him less.

YEAR	TEAM	LVL	AGE	PA	DRC+	VORP	BABIP	BRR	FRAA	WARP
2017	WAS	MLB	28	107	100	9.4	.347	0.3	CF(20): -3.3, LF(5): 0.4	0.1
2018	WAS	MLB	29	370	106	20.8	.364	0.4	RF(67): 5.7, LF(10): -0.5	1.7
2019	WAS	MLB	30	656	102	17.3	.319	3.6	RF(139): 4.3, LF(7): 0.0	2.5
2020	WAS	MLB	31	595	106	18.8	.322	0.9	RF 7, LF 0	2.7

Adam Eaton, continued

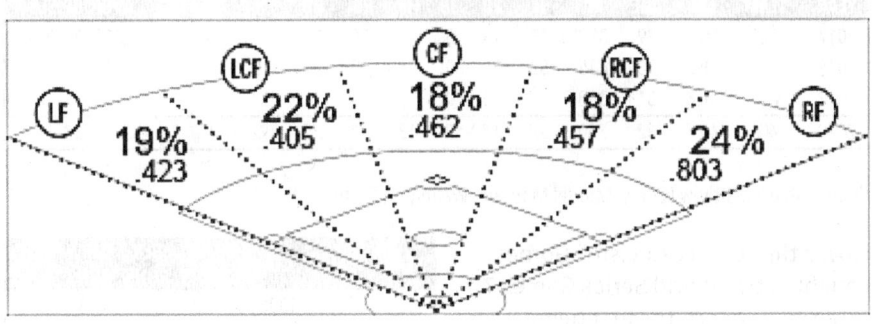

Batted Ball Distribution

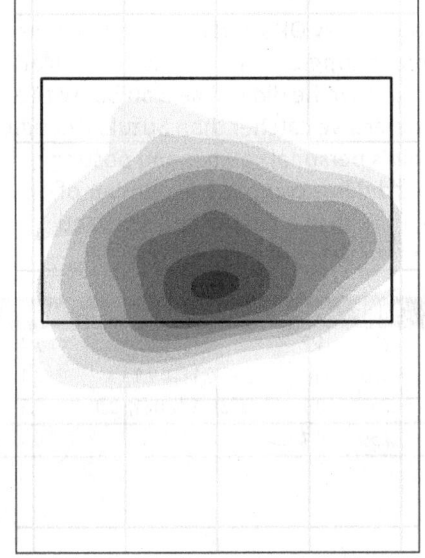

Strike Zone vs LHP

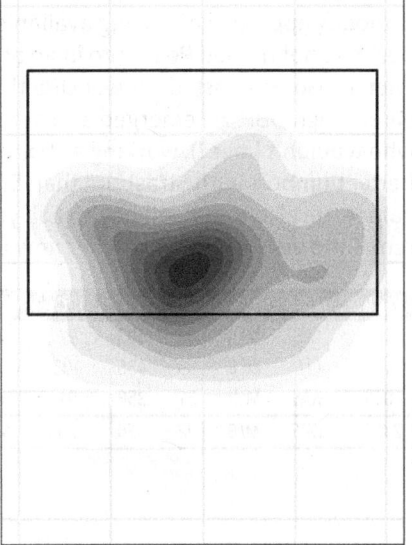

Strike Zone vs RHP

Washington Nationals 2020

Yan Gomes C

Born: 07/19/87   Age: 32   Bats: R   Throws: R
Height: 6'2"   Weight: 215   Origin: Round 10, 2009 Draft (#310 overall)

YEAR	TEAM	LVL	AGE	PA	R	2B	3B	HR	RBI	BB	K	SB	CS	AVG/OBP/SLG
2017	CLE	MLB	29	383	43	15	0	14	56	31	99	0	0	.232/.309/.399
2018	CLE	MLB	30	435	52	26	0	16	48	21	119	0	0	.266/.313/.449
2019	WAS	MLB	31	358	36	16	0	12	43	38	84	2	0	.223/.316/.389
2020	WAS	MLB	32	350	37	16	0	13	43	25	92	1	0	.222/.287/.396

Comparables: Matthew LeCroy, Miguel Montero, Welington Castillo

YEAR	TEAM	P. COUNT	FRM RUNS	BLK RUNS	THRW RUNS	TOT RUNS
2017	CLE	13358	4.2	0.5	2.3	7.6
2018	CLE	15103	7.5	1.7	0.0	9.6
2019	WAS	13260	-4.3	2.8	0.7	-1.0
2020	WAS	14980	-2.0	0.5	0.4	-1.0

How's this for an exorcism? Gomes caught in two World Series Games 7, three years apart, the first being Cleveland's extra-innings loss to the Cubs and the second a late-inning pummeling of the Astros. The Nats acquired Gomes after taking the orthodox approach of sorting available catchers by OPS and then grabbing the best two not named Realmuto in an attempt to upgrade the position from Matt Wieters. Gomes posted a lower OPS this year than he did last season but with a career-high OBP. He emerged as a better defensive catcher than Suzuki (though who wouldn't have?), working as Pat Corbin's personal catcher and posting better numbers with Strasburg than Suzuki did in a comparable number of games. He also remained healthy all year, though in a diminished role, and remains a viable backup catcher now unburdened by the ghosts of 2016.

YEAR	TEAM	LVL	AGE	PA	DRC+	VORP	BABIP	BRR	FRAA	WARP
2017	CLE	MLB	29	383	92	13.6	.283	1.7	C(103): 6.8	2.4
2018	CLE	MLB	30	435	103	22.7	.336	-1.1	C(111): 9.1	3.1
2019	WAS	MLB	31	358	91	14.7	.265	0.1	C(93): -1.6, 1B(1): 0.0	1.3
2020	WAS	MLB	32	350	76	5.6	.268	0.1	C -1	0.4

Yan Gomes, continued

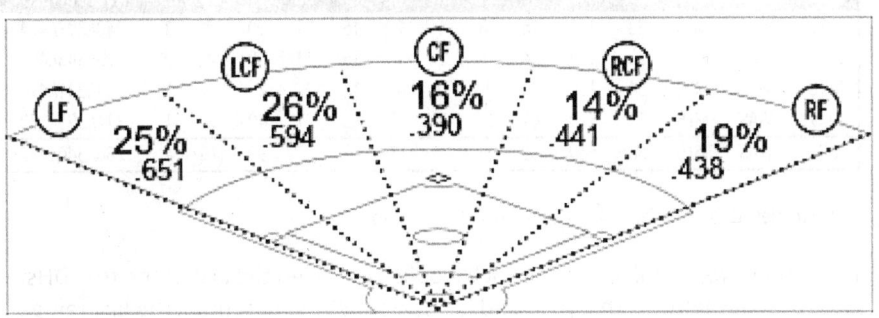

Strike Zone vs LHP　　　　**Strike Zone vs RHP**

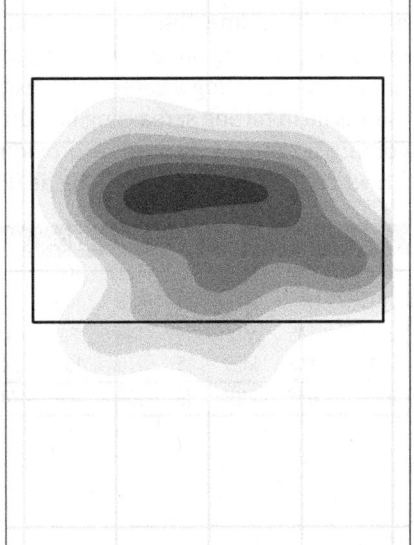

Howie Kendrick INF

Born: 07/12/83 Age: 36 Bats: R Throws: R
Height: 5'11" Weight: 220 Origin: Round 10, 2002 Draft (#294 overall)

YEAR	TEAM	LVL	AGE	PA	R	2B	3B	HR	RBI	BB	K	SB	CS	AVG/OBP/SLG
2017	PHI	MLB	33	156	16	8	1	2	16	11	30	8	3	.340/.397/.454
2017	WAS	MLB	33	178	24	8	2	7	25	11	38	4	2	.293/.343/.494
2018	WAS	MLB	34	160	17	14	0	4	12	5	29	1	1	.303/.331/.474
2019	WAS	MLB	35	370	61	23	1	17	62	27	49	2	1	.344/.395/.572
2020	WAS	MLB	36	560	63	29	2	17	68	37	98	10	4	.286/.340/.447

Comparables: Robinson Canó, Adam Kennedy, Miguel Cairo

In another, worse universe, Kendrick would have been the last of the true DHs. He'll be in his late 30s this year, and is not a great first baseman, the last refuge of old men in the National League. But as every commentator, fellow player and likely, Joe Kelly, in a recurring nightmare he'll have for years, knows: The guy sure can hit. Age is in fact more than a number, and it wasn't clear if and how he'd recover from last year's season-ending Achilles rupture. Surely, he should diminish with time, the numbers said. Instead, he showed increased plate discipline, striking out a hair less than uber-disciplined teammate Anthony Rendon and posting a career-high exit velocity. Even in a juiced ball era, his talents lie in hitting screaming line drives to where fielders aren't. For the coming season, he'll continue providing that pop off the bench and be ready to DH when the rules allow, so long as DH stands for "Dodgers Hurter."

YEAR	TEAM	LVL	AGE	PA	DRC+	VORP	BABIP	BRR	FRAA	WARP
2017	PHI	MLB	33	156	108	10.4	.418	-0.7	LF(24): -0.4, 2B(10): 0.6	0.5
2017	WAS	MLB	33	178	106	10.4	.342	0.6	LF(38): -3.0, 2B(5): -0.2	0.3
2018	WAS	MLB	34	160	94	4.0	.350	-3.1	2B(33): -2.7, LF(6): -0.1	-0.2
2019	WAS	MLB	35	370	132	24.9	.359	-2.6	1B(48): 1.8, 2B(23): 0.7	2.3
2020	WAS	MLB	36	560	106	14.1	.325	-2.5	1B 7, 2B 0	2.2

Howie Kendrick, continued

Batted Ball Distribution

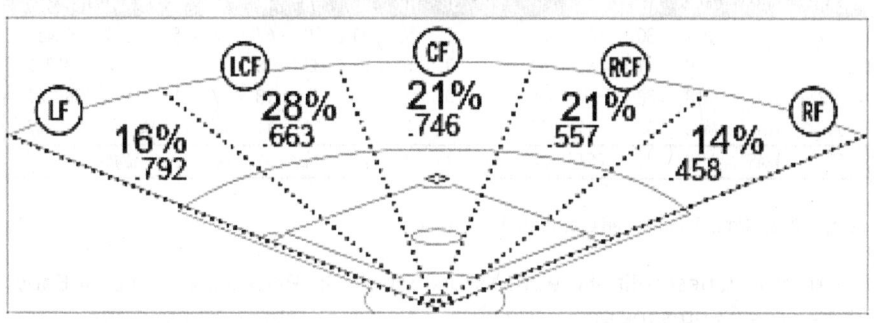

Strike Zone vs LHP   Strike Zone vs RHP

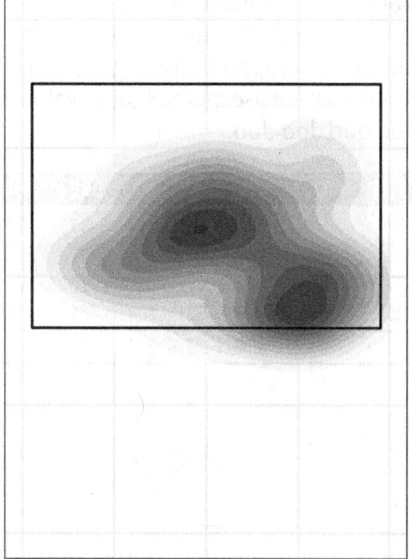

Gerardo Parra OF

Born: 05/06/87 Age: 33 Bats: L Throws: L
Height: 5'11" Weight: 210 Origin: International Free Agent, 2004

YEAR	TEAM	LVL	AGE	PA	R	2B	3B	HR	RBI	BB	K	SB	CS	AVG/OBP/SLG
2017	COL	MLB	30	425	56	24	1	10	71	20	67	2	5	.309/.341/.452
2018	COL	MLB	31	443	52	17	0	6	53	32	75	11	4	.284/.342/.372
2019	SFN	MLB	32	97	8	3	0	1	6	8	18	2	1	.198/.278/.267
2019	WAS	MLB	32	204	30	11	1	8	42	11	41	6	2	.250/.300/.447
2020	WAS	MLB	33	251	24	12	1	6	27	14	51	4	2	.240/.290/.378

Comparables: Omar Infante, Carl Crawford, Thad Bosley

The dumbest, best split of the 2019 season has to be Parra's pre- and post-Baby Shark-as-walk-up-song one. Parra posted a barely-keeping-his-head-above-water slash line of .209/.276/.331 before June 19—the day of that fateful music change—and a .262/.314/.460 one after, enough to keep him swimming along in the majors, in addition to the chummier atmosphere he brought to the Nationals clubhouse. As a Nat, he matched offensive wits with Matt Adams and Victor Robles, provided some additional outfield depth and irritated the heck out of the Dodgers in the regular season, all of which might have made him the Nationals' least-expected most-valuable catch. His next stop? N-P-B, doo doo doo doo doo doo.

YEAR	TEAM	LVL	AGE	PA	DRC+	VORP	BABIP	BRR	FRAA	WARP
2017	COL	MLB	30	425	99	9.4	.343	-2.5	LF(82): 3.6, RF(22): -0.1	1.1
2018	COL	MLB	31	443	96	11.2	.334	3.3	LF(111): 6.8, RF(10): 1.9	2.1
2019	SFN	MLB	32	97	78	0.0	.235	0.6	LF(20): 2.2, RF(11): 3.5	0.6
2019	WAS	MLB	32	204	84	1.0	.279	1.7	RF(23): 0.5, 1B(14): 0.6	0.4
2020	WAS	MLB	33	251	75	0.7	.282	0.6	LF 3, RF 1	0.4

Gerardo Parra, continued

Batted Ball Distribution

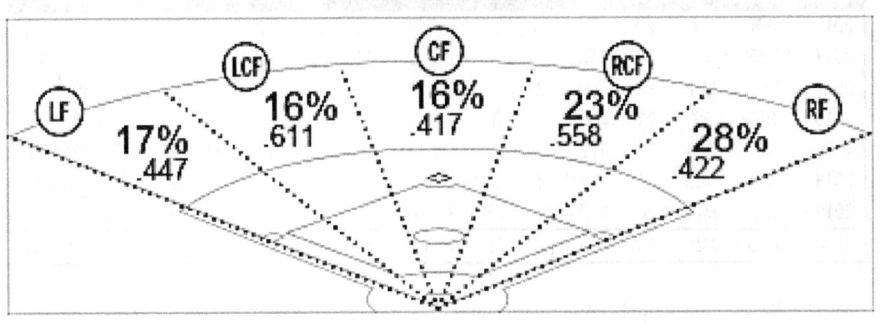

Strike Zone vs LHP　　　**Strike Zone vs RHP**

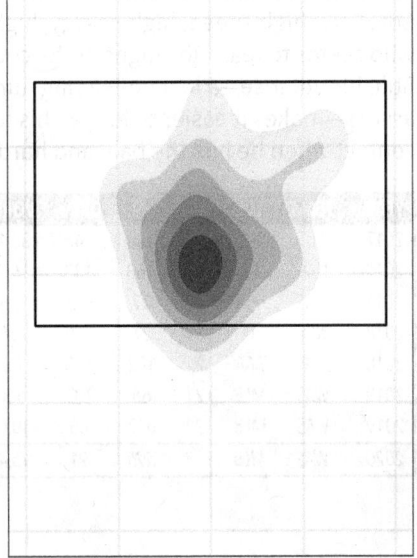

Washington Nationals 2020

Victor Robles   CF

Born: 05/19/97   Age: 23   Bats: R   Throws: R
Height: 6'0"   Weight: 190   Origin: International Free Agent, 2013

YEAR	TEAM	LVL	AGE	PA	R	2B	3B	HR	RBI	BB	K	SB	CS	AVG/OBP/SLG
2017	POT	A+	20	338	49	25	7	7	33	25	62	16	7	.289/.377/.495
2017	HAR	AA	20	158	24	12	1	3	14	12	22	11	3	.324/.394/.489
2017	WAS	MLB	20	27	2	1	2	0	4	0	6	0	1	.250/.308/.458
2018	NAT	RK	21	27	7	1	0	0	1	7	4	4	1	.333/.556/.389
2018	SYR	AAA	21	182	25	9	1	2	10	18	26	14	6	.278/.356/.386
2018	WAS	MLB	21	66	8	3	1	3	10	4	12	3	2	.288/.348/.525
2019	WAS	MLB	22	617	86	33	3	17	65	35	140	28	9	.255/.326/.419
2020	WAS	MLB	23	595	66	28	4	17	68	35	132	24	9	.247/.320/.410

Comparables: Manuel Margot, Justin Upton, Ruben Sierra

Let's all lean into Robles the way Robles leans into pitches. Robles would be the most exciting young gun on the Nationals if not for his younger, better counterpart in left field. He's a rookie in the way that young players (other than Soto) are: high speed, high energy, high swing rate on pitches outside the zone, who seems to learn throughout the course of each game only to reset the next. Still, his defense—a league-leading number of centerfield putouts and assists—makes it easier to forgive his tendency to get on base through soft contact when he hits the ball, and hard contact when the ball hits him.

YEAR	TEAM	LVL	AGE	PA	DRC+	VORP	BABIP	BRR	FRAA	WARP
2017	POT	A+	20	338	148	30.1	.345	0.7	CF(77): 16.1	4.5
2017	HAR	AA	20	158	138	16.7	.368	2.7	CF(31): 4.1, LF(3): -0.1	1.9
2017	WAS	MLB	20	27	79	-0.6	.333	-0.8	RF(6): 1.2, CF(3): -0.3	0.0
2018	NAT	RK	21	27	199	4.7	.429	1.9	CF(7): -0.3	0.5
2018	SYR	AAA	21	182	100	9.8	.318	1.2	CF(39): -0.8	0.6
2018	WAS	MLB	21	66	103	5.3	.311	0.7	CF(14): 0.1, LF(2): 0.0	0.3
2019	WAS	MLB	22	617	85	10.0	.310	5.6	CF(141): 6.6, RF(15): 1.1	2.3
2020	WAS	MLB	23	595	91	18.4	.297	2.9	CF 9	2.8

Victor Robles, continued

Batted Ball Distribution

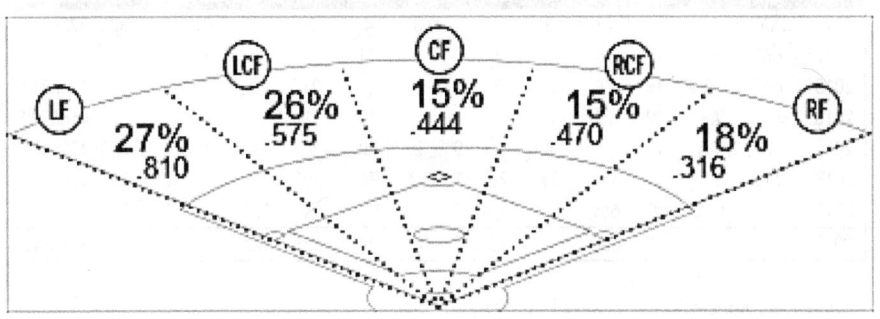

Strike Zone vs LHP   **Strike Zone vs RHP**

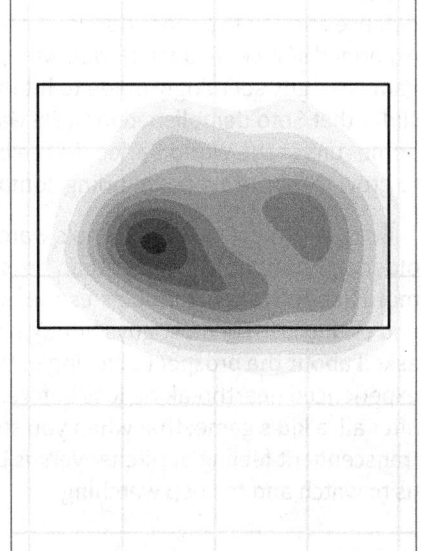

Juan Soto LF

Born: 10/25/98   Age: 21   Bats: L   Throws: L
Height: 6'1"   Weight: 185   Origin: International Free Agent, 2015

YEAR	TEAM	LVL	AGE	PA	R	2B	3B	HR	RBI	BB	K	SB	CS	AVG/OBP/SLG
2017	NAT	RK	18	27	3	1	1	0	4	2	1	0	0	.320/.370/.440
2017	HAG	A	18	96	15	5	0	3	14	10	8	1	2	.360/.427/.523
2018	HAG	A	19	74	12	5	3	5	24	14	13	2	0	.373/.486/.814
2018	POT	A+	19	73	17	3	1	7	18	11	8	0	1	.371/.466/.790
2018	HAR	AA	19	35	4	2	0	2	10	4	7	1	0	.323/.400/.581
2018	WAS	MLB	19	494	77	25	1	22	70	79	99	5	2	.292/.406/.517
2019	WAS	MLB	20	659	110	32	5	34	110	108	132	12	1	.282/.401/.548
2020	WAS	MLB	21	630	92	30	3	35	102	85	123	5	2	.284/.382/.543

Comparables: Ronald Acuña Jr., Mike Trout, Tony Conigliaro

Talk about adjustments. Soto spent the year adjusting to pitchers who served him a steady diet of breaking stuff—with apologies to last year's Annual, sliders are one of the few things he doesn't routinely crush. To left field, improving his defense enough to get a Gold Glove nod. To a two-strike count with an expanded stance. To Josh Hader, who dished up a high fastball in the Wild Card game to a guy seemingly made to hit them. To Clayton Kershaw, who threw a slider that Soto demolished in NLDS Game 5. To Gerrit Cole, off whom he hit two home runs in the World Series. To the biggest stage in the world, talent seeming to grow to fill the ever-expanding container it's in.

Soto, as almost everyone who's watched him take a pitch knows, plays both older and somehow younger than he is. He's patient, with a swing profile that's more Rendon-ish than Robles-esque, watching balls go by with the excitement and enthusiasm of most guys hitting one over the fence. Younger too—when asked about the prospect of losing in the World Series, Soto remarked he'd experienced heartbreaking loss before…in Little League. A reminder that this is, after all, a kid's game; that when you strip away the pomp and ceremony, it's the transcendent feeling of pitcher versus batter, defense versus offense, that drives us to watch and to keep watching.

YEAR	TEAM	LVL	AGE	PA	DRC+	VORP	BABIP	BRR	FRAA	WARP
2017	NAT	RK	18	27	135	1.5	.333	0.0	RF(9): -1.1	0.0
2017	HAG	A	18	96	181	8.0	.373	1.0	RF(19): -1.9, LF(2): -0.3	0.9
2018	HAG	A	19	74	222	14.5	.405	0.3	RF(14): 1.1, CF(2): 0.2	1.2
2018	POT	A+	19	73	260	15.4	.340	1.4	RF(14): 1.0, LF(1): 0.0	1.6
2018	HAR	AA	19	35	113	3.6	.364	0.0	LF(4): 0.6, RF(4): -0.5	0.1
2018	WAS	MLB	19	494	125	40.5	.338	-0.5	LF(114): 2.7	3.0
2019	WAS	MLB	20	659	136	49.0	.312	1.4	LF(150): -0.8	4.9
2020	WAS	MLB	21	630	133	43.6	.310	-0.1	LF 3	4.8

Juan Soto, continued

Batted Ball Distribution

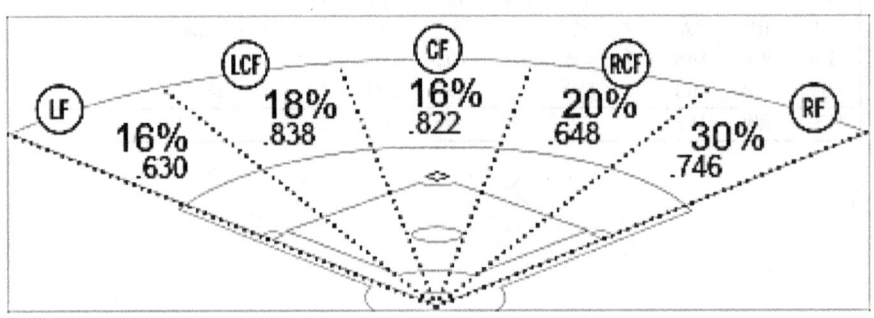

Strike Zone vs LHP **Strike Zone vs RHP**

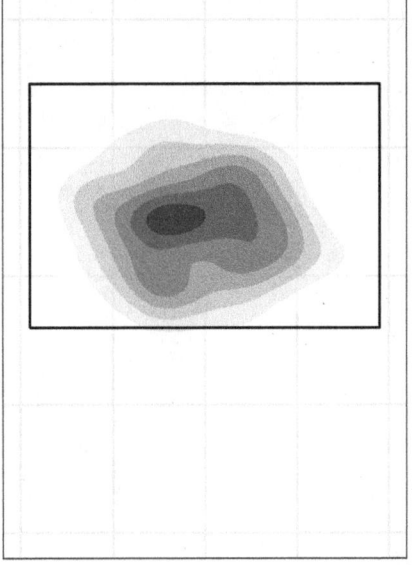

Kurt Suzuki C

Born: 10/04/83   Age: 36   Bats: R   Throws: R
Height: 5'11"   Weight: 210   Origin: Round 2, 2004 Draft (#67 overall)

YEAR	TEAM	LVL	AGE	PA	R	2B	3B	HR	RBI	BB	K	SB	CS	AVG/OBP/SLG
2017	ATL	MLB	33	309	38	13	0	19	50	17	39	0	0	.283/.351/.536
2018	ATL	MLB	34	388	45	24	0	12	50	22	43	0	0	.271/.332/.444
2019	WAS	MLB	35	309	37	11	0	17	63	20	36	0	1	.264/.324/.486
2020	WAS	MLB	36	301	35	15	0	13	40	18	42	0	0	.256/.316/.448

Comparables: Rick Cerone, Ramon Hernandez, Brian Schneider

There's something to be said for distance. The sixty feet and six inches from the mound to the plate. The distance from the stands to the field. The distance between who we feel players are and who they ought to be. We could talk about Suzuki's offensive output; he posted the sixth-highest DRC+ among catchers who started more than 50 games. Or his work in game planning with Scherzer, Strasburg and Sánchez. His 2012 assurance to Doolittle to trust his fastball. But overshadowing all of that was the post-World Series trip to the White House, the seeming unawareness that his actions—donning a MAGA hat and literally being embraced by Trump—have consequences on others, one that left many Nationals fans feeling not just distant, but unmoored, adrift from a once-beloved fan favorite.

YEAR	TEAM	P. COUNT	FRM RUNS	BLK RUNS	THRW RUNS	TOT RUNS
2017	ATL	10594	-0.6	1.4	-0.9	-0.7
2018	ATL	12497	-7.5	1.5	-0.4	-6.6
2019	WAS	10602	-5.9	-1.7	-1.3	-9.3
2020	WAS	13270	-7.1	-0.1	-1.4	-8.6

YEAR	TEAM	LVL	AGE	PA	DRC+	VORP	BABIP	BRR	FRAA	WARP
2017	ATL	MLB	33	309	129	27.1	.268	-2.8	C(77): 1.9	2.6
2018	ATL	MLB	34	388	115	25.9	.275	-2.0	C(93): -5.5	1.8
2019	WAS	MLB	35	309	115	22.3	.248	0.4	C(75): -8.6	1.4
2020	WAS	MLB	36	301	96	11.8	.262	-0.9	C -8	0.4

Washington Nationals 2020

Kurt Suzuki, continued

Batted Ball Distribution

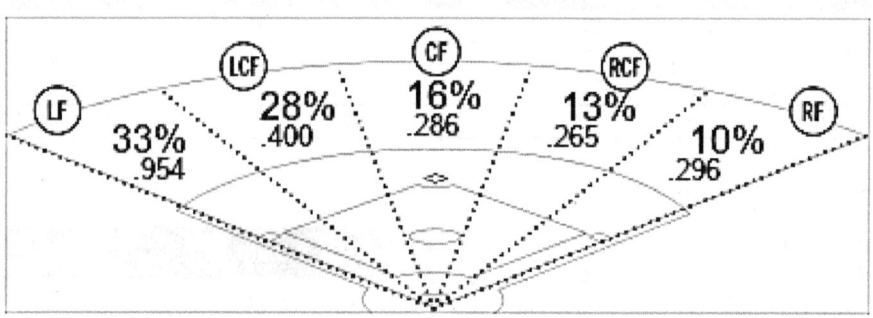

LF	LCF	CF	RCF	RF
33% .954	28% .400	16% .286	13% .265	10% .296

Strike Zone vs LHP **Strike Zone vs RHP**

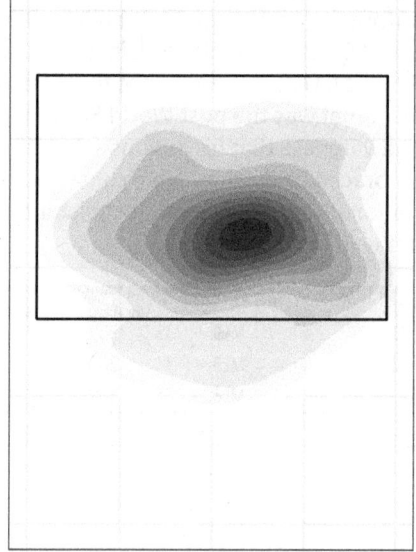

Eric Thames 1B

Born: 11/10/86   Age: 33   Bats: L   Throws: R
Height: 6'0"   Weight: 210   Origin: Round 7, 2008 Draft (#219 overall)

YEAR	TEAM	LVL	AGE	PA	R	2B	3B	HR	RBI	BB	K	SB	CS	AVG/OBP/SLG
2017	MIL	MLB	30	551	83	26	4	31	63	75	163	4	2	.247/.359/.518
2018	MIL	MLB	31	278	41	10	3	16	37	29	97	7	0	.219/.306/.478
2019	MIL	MLB	32	459	67	23	2	25	61	51	140	3	2	.247/.346/.505
2020	WAS	MLB	33	251	35	12	1	15	40	28	80	3	1	.249/.344/.517

Comparables: Brandon Moss, Carlos Delgado, Brad Wilkerson

Three years into Thames's return to American baseball, we can safely say what you see is what you'll get. His swing features too many holes to avoid an abhorrent 30-percent strikeout rate, but he is disciplined enough to take his walks and has undeniable power. The biggest problem, honestly, is his defensive incompetence. His walk-and-bop stylings at the dish would enable him to start most days if he was a passable corner outfielder. But his bat loses some of its value when he's limited to either first base or DH. Is it any wonder, then, why the Brewers elected to bid him adieu?

YEAR	TEAM	LVL	AGE	PA	DRC+	VORP	BABIP	BRR	FRAA	WARP
2017	MIL	MLB	30	551	117	28.8	.309	-2.7	1B(108): -2.2, LF(25): -1.8	1.4
2018	MIL	MLB	31	278	96	14.0	.284	2.3	RF(31): -0.3, 1B(29): -0.9	0.6
2019	MIL	MLB	32	459	112	15.3	.313	1.8	1B(105): -1.4, RF(12): -0.1	1.5
2020	WAS	MLB	33	251	114	13.0	.321	0.1	1B 0, RF 0	1.4

Eric Thames, continued

Batted Ball Distribution

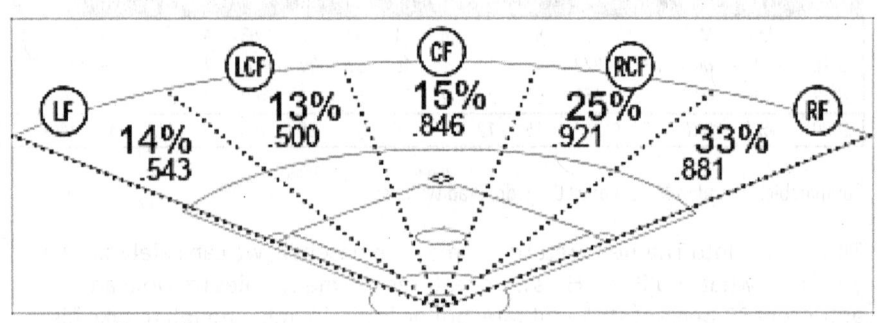

Strike Zone vs LHP   **Strike Zone vs RHP**

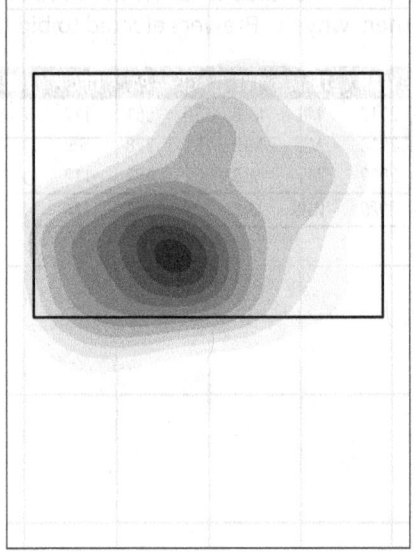

Trea Turner SS

Born: 06/30/93 Age: 27 Bats: R Throws: R
Height: 6'2" Weight: 185 Origin: Round 1, 2014 Draft (#13 overall)

YEAR	TEAM	LVL	AGE	PA	R	2B	3B	HR	RBI	BB	K	SB	CS	AVG/OBP/SLG
2017	WAS	MLB	24	447	75	24	6	11	45	30	80	46	8	.284/.338/.451
2018	WAS	MLB	25	740	103	27	6	19	73	69	132	43	9	.271/.344/.416
2019	WAS	MLB	26	569	96	37	5	19	57	43	113	35	5	.298/.353/.497
2020	WAS	MLB	27	595	71	31	6	19	75	46	120	36	8	.281/.340/.465

Comparables: Juan Samuel, Gordon Beckham, Tony Batista

It turns out that 85 percent of Turner is still a good amount of Trea. The shortstop took a pitch off his hand on April 3rd, a bunt attempt on a ball that ran in on him, leaving one and a half of his fingers broken all season. He initially thought they were merely dislocated and allegedly told training staff to, "pop that [expletive] back in." So, operating at 85 percent would explain some of the defensive miscues, including an FRAA around half of his 2018 level. (Though not being next to a defensive black hole in the form of 2018 Daniel Murphy likely helped with that.) He didn't suffer as much on the other side of the plate, where he employed an 8.5-finger grip, trading a slightly elevated strikeout rate and chasing more out of the zone for an increase in both average and power. He'll have a shortened offseason in which to heal, but should consider retaining his altered grip, even at 100 percent.

YEAR	TEAM	LVL	AGE	PA	DRC+	VORP	BABIP	BRR	FRAA	WARP
2017	WAS	MLB	24	447	99	36.6	.329	6.8	SS(95): 0.2	2.7
2018	WAS	MLB	25	740	107	46.5	.314	2.7	SS(159): 7.1	5.0
2019	WAS	MLB	26	569	108	33.4	.348	4.1	SS(122): 3.8	4.0
2020	WAS	MLB	27	595	109	32.4	.330	2.5	SS 6	3.9

Trea Turner, continued

Batted Ball Distribution

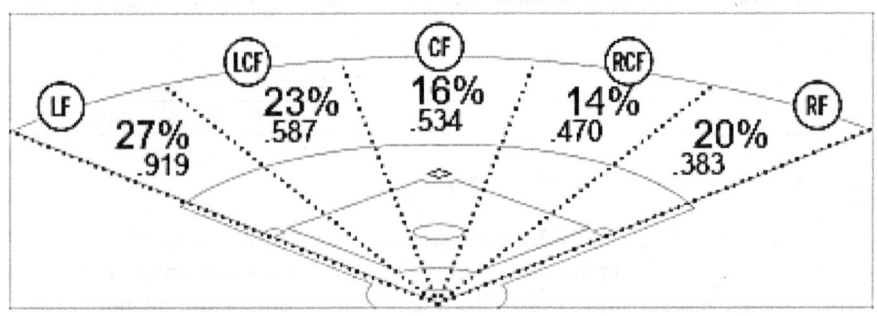

Strike Zone vs LHP   **Strike Zone vs RHP**

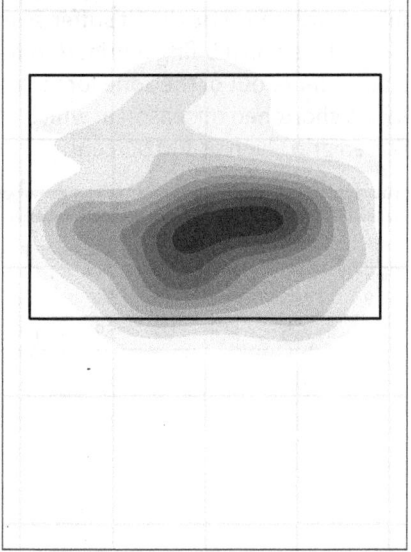

Ryan Zimmerman 1B

Born: 09/28/84 Age: 35 Bats: R Throws: R
Height: 6'3" Weight: 215 Origin: Round 1, 2005 Draft (#4 overall)

YEAR	TEAM	LVL	AGE	PA	R	2B	3B	HR	RBI	BB	K	SB	CS	AVG/OBP/SLG
2017	WAS	MLB	32	576	90	33	0	36	108	44	126	1	0	.303/.358/.573
2018	WAS	MLB	33	323	33	21	2	13	51	30	55	1	1	.264/.337/.486
2019	WAS	MLB	34	190	20	9	0	6	27	17	39	0	0	.257/.321/.415
2020	WAS	MLB	35	251	29	14	0	10	33	20	56	1	0	.249/.314/.443

Comparables: Alex Gordon, Larry Parrish, Ed Sprague

There's a certain space in baseball mythology reserved not for the All-Stars or the has-beens, but something rarer and more fraught: the could-have-beens. Zimmerman's potential has been hanging over him like a cluster of grapes above Tantalus—something we all can see but that, frustratingly, remained just out of his grasp. He's been at this for 15 years, drafted when Soto was a kindergartener, a face-of-the-franchise player for a team that wasted six of his best years finding its footing. He missed much of the season with a foot injury, plantar fasciitis, that kind of nagging thing that sets in in your mid-30s and never really departs. But whatever gods or monsters control baseball's narrative, whatever forces decide who feasts and who stays hungry, wrote Zimmerman a happy ending—reaching up and grabbing hold of the success that had eluded him for so long.

YEAR	TEAM	LVL	AGE	PA	DRC+	VORP	BABIP	BRR	FRAA	WARP
2017	WAS	MLB	32	576	130	39.4	.335	-0.3	1B(143): -11.4	1.8
2018	WAS	MLB	33	323	111	14.5	.284	-0.5	1B(73): 1.4	1.0
2019	WAS	MLB	34	190	93	1.4	.297	-0.9	1B(44): 1.2	0.2
2020	WAS	MLB	35	251	98	7.3	.288	-0.3	1B 0	0.7

Ryan Zimmerman, continued

Batted Ball Distribution

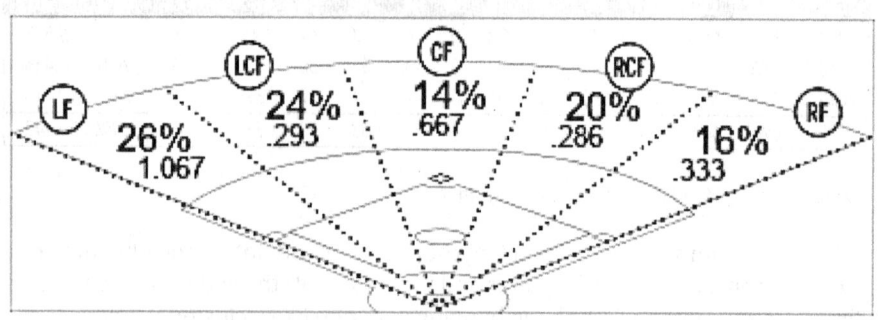

Strike Zone vs LHP   **Strike Zone vs RHP**

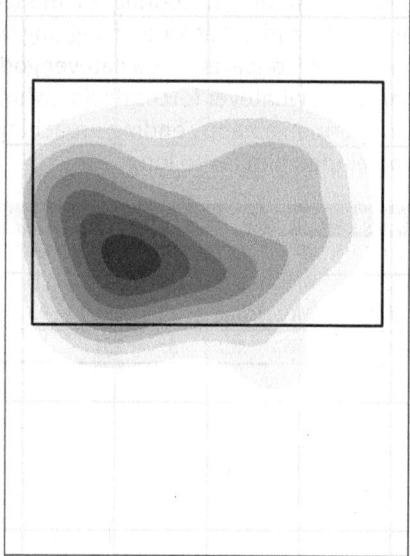

Fernando Abad LHP

Born: 12/17/85   Age: 34   Bats: L   Throws: L
Height: 6'1"   Weight: 220   Origin: International Free Agent, 2002

YEAR	TEAM	LVL	AGE	W	L	SV	G	GS	IP	H	HR	BB/9	K/9	K	GB%	BABIP
2017	BOS	MLB	31	2	1	1	48	0	43²	40	4	2.9	7.6	37	46%	.286
2019	RIC	AA	33	1	0	0	3	0	6	3	0	1.5	9.0	6	27%	.200
2019	SAC	AAA	33	2	3	13	38	0	44	49	3	0.8	10.0	49	47%	.357
2019	SFN	MLB	33	0	2	0	21	0	13	9	2	2.1	6.2	9	62%	.200
2020	WAS	MLB	34	2	2	0	33	0	35	37	5	2.9	8.5	33	44%	.314

Comparables: Dan Jennings, Mike Stanton, Jerry Blevins

After a brief sojourn to rip up the Atlantic League in 2018, Abad picked up right where he left off in affiliated baseball this past season: he worked his way back up to the majors where he beat up left-handed hitters and barely skated by the righties. The stuff remains roughly the same as it always has, which means his profile does too: He's exactly the kind of relief pitcher teams want waiting in Triple-A, or on standby as the third left-hander out of the bullpen. Sure, they're constantly looking for an upgrade over guys like this, but every team needs a reliever or two like him, nominative determinism be damned.

YEAR	TEAM	LVL	AGE	WHIP	ERA	DRA	WARP	MPH	FB%	WHF	CSP
2017	BOS	MLB	31	1.24	3.30	5.11	0.0	94.4	53.7	7.7	43.2
2019	RIC	AA	33	0.67	0.00	3.08	0.1				
2019	SAC	AAA	33	1.20	3.07	3.04	1.4				
2019	SFN	MLB	33	0.92	4.15	4.28	0.2	95.1	57.9	10.5	48.3
2020	WAS	MLB	34	1.38	4.40	4.80	0.2	93.5	54	8.4	45.7

Washington Nationals 2020

Fernando Abad, continued

Pitch Shape vs LHH

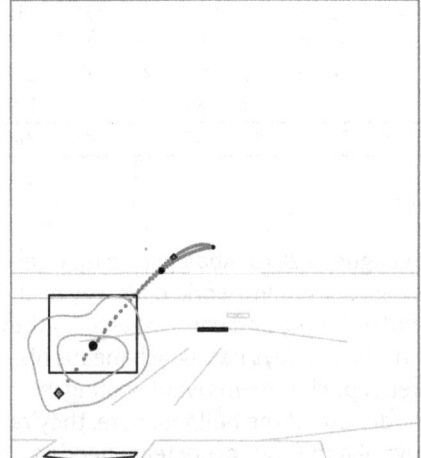

Pitch Shape vs RHH

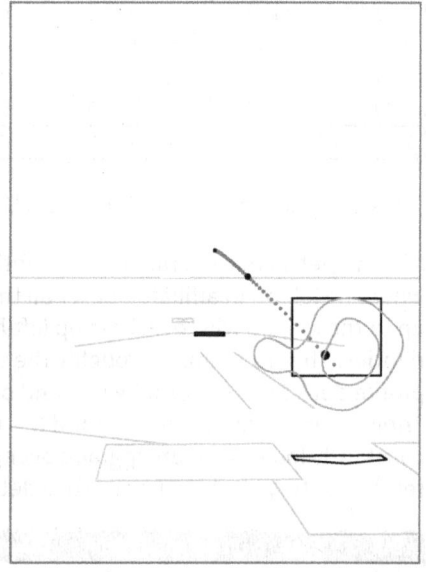

Type	Frequency	Velocity	H Movement	V Movement
● Fastball	57.9%	93.2 [102]	12.1 [77]	-19.5 [91]
☐ Sinker				
+ Cutter				
▲ Changeup	14.0%	76 [66]	8.5 [113]	-33 [84]
✕ Splitter				
▽ Slider				
◇ Curveball	28.1%	78.6 [100]	-4.7 [89]	-48 [99]
✦ Slow Curveball				
✱ Knuckleball				
▼ Screwball				

Patrick Corbin   LHP

Born: 07/19/89   Age: 30   Bats: L   Throws: L
Height: 6'3"   Weight: 210   Origin: Round 2, 2009 Draft (#80 overall)

YEAR	TEAM	LVL	AGE	W	L	SV	G	GS	IP	H	HR	BB/9	K/9	K	GB%	BABIP
2017	ARI	MLB	27	14	13	0	33	32	189^2	208	26	2.9	8.4	178	52%	.326
2018	ARI	MLB	28	11	7	0	33	33	200	162	15	2.2	11.1	246	49%	.302
2019	WAS	MLB	29	14	7	0	33	33	202	169	24	3.1	10.6	238	51%	.290
2020	WAS	MLB	30	11	9	0	29	29	175	161	22	3.2	10.7	209	51%	.314

Comparables: Kevin Gausman, Travis Wood, Jaime García

If 2019 Nationals starting pitching was a gauntlet, specifically the Infinity Gauntlet, Corbin was the Soul Gem, seeming to steal, control and manipulate hitters' spirits. Corbin had a top-15 DRA, a top-10 WARP and was still the third-best starting pitcher on his own team. When his slider snaps, it's basically the Thanos of pitches—it generates more than a 50 percent whiff-per-swing rate, and he deploys it on a two-strike count more than half the time. The kind of put-away pitch that feels inevitable, and still brings hitters to their knees chasing it. He also threw a slow-as-you-please curve to righties this year, possible proof the soul of Liván Hernández remains in Nationals Park.

YEAR	TEAM	LVL	AGE	WHIP	ERA	DRA	WARP	MPH	FB%	WHF	CSP
2017	ARI	MLB	27	1.42	4.03	4.92	1.4	94.5	53.3	11.9	43.8
2018	ARI	MLB	28	1.05	3.15	2.74	5.9	93.9	48.6	16.3	41.6
2019	WAS	MLB	29	1.18	3.25	3.09	5.9	94.3	53.6	14.9	42.2
2020	WAS	MLB	30	1.27	3.71	3.72	4.1	93.5	51.7	14.6	42.3

Washington Nationals 2020

Patrick Corbin, continued

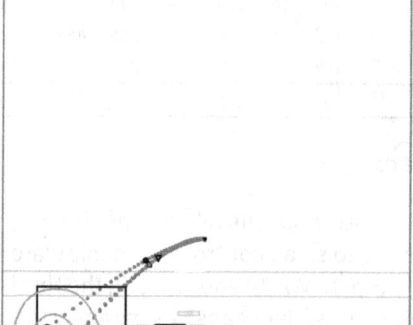
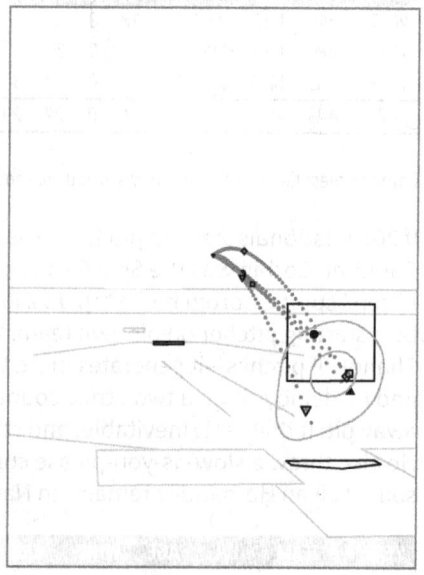

Type	Frequency	Velocity	H Movement	V Movement
● Fastball	18.9%	92.3 [100]	7.9 [95]	-15.1 [102]
□ Sinker	34.7%	92.2 [98]	13.3 [96]	-19.2 [104]
+ Cutter				
▲ Changeup	5.8%	82.1 [89]	9.7 [107]	-27.1 [101]
✕ Splitter				
▽ Slider	37.0%	82 [90]	-2.9 [91]	-36.7 [90]
◇ Curveball	3.6%	68.3 [66]	-2.6 [80]	-53 [88]
✦ Slow Curveball				
✳ Knuckleball				
▼ Screwball				

Sean Doolittle   LHP

Born: 09/26/86   Age: 33   Bats: L   Throws: L
Height: 6'2"   Weight: 204   Origin: Round 1, 2007 Draft (#41 overall)

YEAR	TEAM	LVL	AGE	W	L	SV	G	GS	IP	H	HR	BB/9	K/9	K	GB%	BABIP
2017	OAK	MLB	30	1	0	3	23	0	21¹	12	3	0.8	13.1	31	37%	.209
2017	WAS	MLB	30	1	0	21	30	0	30	22	2	2.4	9.3	31	28%	.260
2018	WAS	MLB	31	3	3	25	43	0	45	21	3	1.2	12.0	60	33%	.196
2019	WAS	MLB	32	6	5	29	63	0	60	63	11	2.2	9.9	66	27%	.313
2020	WAS	MLB	33	3	2	32	49	0	52	44	9	2.0	9.9	57	27%	.270

Comparables: Jake McGee, Nick Vincent, Rafael Soriano

If you're in DC and looking for a great lefty independent bookstore experience, look no further than Doolittle's. While other stores in the area floundered—Rosenthal's, for instance, held an early season fire-sale before closing to spend more time with its inventory—Doolittle's shouldered much of the workload, at times serving as the only reliable purveyor of outs in the area. This rapid expansion in role before the arrival of Rodney's, a traveling library, and Hudson's, which survived two renovations in its main wing, led to near-constant operating hours. After a much-needed rest and restock, the store has regained its reliable collection of high, unhittable fastballs. Also, as you'd expect, it's very pet friendly.

YEAR	TEAM	LVL	AGE	WHIP	ERA	DRA	WARP	MPH	FB%	WHF	CSP
2017	OAK	MLB	30	0.66	3.38	2.95	0.5	96.3	87.9	17.5	44.5
2017	WAS	MLB	30	1.00	2.40	3.71	0.5	96.5	87.5	16.8	48.3
2018	WAS	MLB	31	0.60	1.60	2.99	1.0	96.3	88.6	18.9	50.7
2019	WAS	MLB	32	1.30	4.05	4.88	0.3	95.6	88.2	13.9	50.8
2020	WAS	MLB	33	1.08	3.29	3.46	1.1	94.9	87.1	15.6	49.2

Washington Nationals 2020

Sean Doolittle, continued

Pitch Shape vs LHH　　　　**Pitch Shape vs RHH**

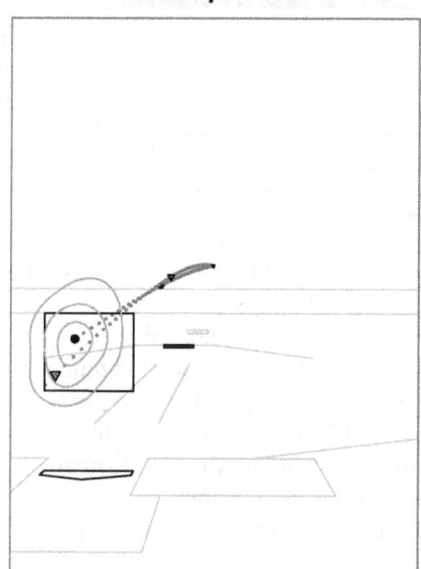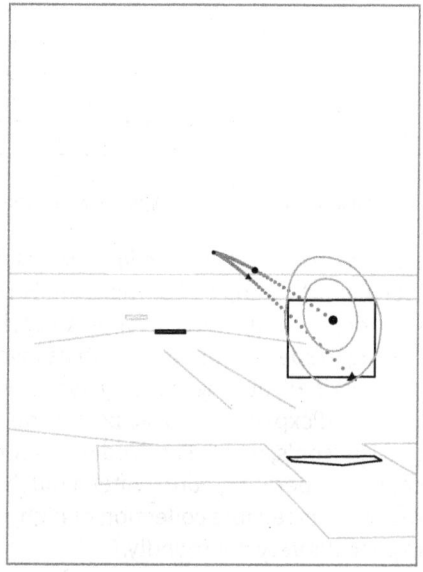

Type	Frequency	Velocity	H Movement	V Movement
● Fastball	88.2%	93.8 [104]	3.6 [115]	-10.6 [114]
☐ Sinker				
+ Cutter				
▲ Changeup	6.1%	84 [95]	12.3 [95]	-20.6 [120]
✕ Splitter				
▽ Slider	5.8%	81.2 [87]	-7.3 [109]	-34.4 [96]
◇ Curveball				
✦ Slow Curveball				
✱ Knuckleball				
▼ Screwball				

Roenis Elías LHP

Born: 08/01/88   Age: 31   Bats: L   Throws: L
Height: 6'1"   Weight: 205   Origin: International Free Agent, 2011

YEAR	TEAM	LVL	AGE	W	L	SV	G	GS	IP	H	HR	BB/9	K/9	K	GB%	BABIP
2017	PAW	AAA	28	1	4	0	7	7	34	43	9	2.4	6.6	25	33%	.312
2017	BOS	MLB	28	0	0	0	1	0	0^1	0	0	27.0	27.0	1	0%	.000
2018	PAW	AAA	29	1	0	1	4	0	7^1	2	1	2.5	11.0	9	47%	.071
2018	TAC	AAA	29	2	4	0	10	7	33^2	32	1	4.0	8.3	31	44%	.313
2018	SEA	MLB	29	3	1	0	23	4	51	46	1	2.8	6.0	34	35%	.285
2019	SEA	MLB	30	4	2	14	44	0	47	41	8	3.3	8.6	45	36%	.250
2019	WAS	MLB	30	0	0	0	4	0	3	5	2	3.0	6.0	2	30%	.375
2020	WAS	MLB	31	2	2	0	39	0	42	41	7	3.3	8.3	38	37%	.293

Comparables: Shane Greene, Sean Gilmartin, Joe Kelly

The Nationals began the season with three bullpen lefties in Sipp, Grace and Doolittle. By September, only one remained. Elías was meant to be part of a solution to the chronic-lack-of-lefties woes. Instead, he posted bad reverse splits, a change from previous seasons, including an OPS above 1000 against left-handed batters mostly due to his curveball going from nigh unhittable by lefties to just nigh. Add to that his hamstring troubles—some brought on by attempting do something a former AL relief pitcher should never do: swing a bat—and the Nats had no choice but to leave him behind.

YEAR	TEAM	LVL	AGE	WHIP	ERA	DRA	WARP	MPH	FB%	WHF	CSP
2017	PAW	AAA	28	1.53	6.62	6.56	-0.3				
2017	BOS	MLB	28	3.00	0.00	1.45	0.0	93.6	54.6	18.2	36.5
2018	PAW	AAA	29	0.55	1.23	2.38	0.3				
2018	TAC	AAA	29	1.40	4.54	4.60	0.3				
2018	SEA	MLB	29	1.22	2.65	5.35	-0.2	96.0	55	9.8	46.9
2019	SEA	MLB	30	1.23	3.64	5.00	0.2	95.9	57.3	13	50.8
2019	WAS	MLB	30	2.00	9.00	12.80	-0.2	95.7	60	10	56.2
2020	WAS	MLB	31	1.36	4.66	4.59	0.4	95.1	56	11.4	45.8

Roenis Elías, continued

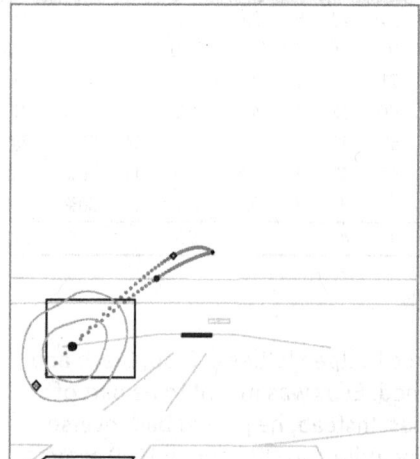
Pitch Shape vs LHH

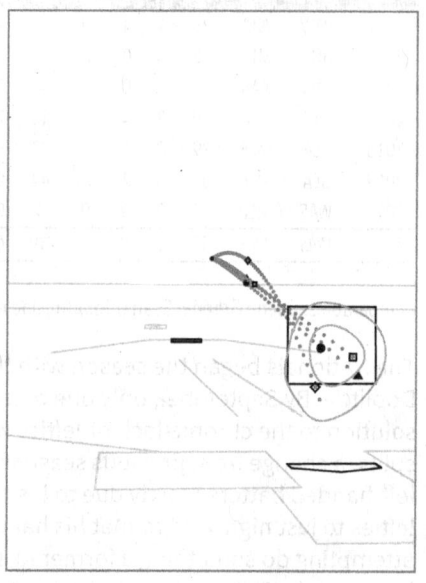
Pitch Shape vs RHH

Type	Frequency	Velocity	H Movement	V Movement
● Fastball	52.7%	94.3 [105]	8.3 [94]	-12.2 [110]
☐ Sinker	4.8%	94.2 [108]	14.2 [90]	-15.7 [116]
+ Cutter				
▲ Changeup	29.2%	87 [106]	16 [78]	-25.5 [106]
✕ Splitter				
▽ Slider				
◇ Curveball	13.3%	77.9 [98]	-13.4 [124]	-52.2 [90]
✦ Slow Curveball				
✱ Knuckleball				
▼ Screwball				

Erick Fedde   RHP

Born: 02/25/93   Age: 27   Bats: R   Throws: R
Height: 6'4"   Weight: 195   Origin: Round 1, 2014 Draft (#18 overall)

YEAR	TEAM	LVL	AGE	W	L	SV	G	GS	IP	H	HR	BB/9	K/9	K	GB%	BABIP
2017	HAR	AA	24	3	3	0	17	7	56^1	45	4	2.9	8.6	54	52%	.272
2017	SYR	AAA	24	1	2	0	12	6	34	37	3	1.3	6.6	25	62%	.315
2017	WAS	MLB	24	0	1	0	3	3	15^1	25	5	4.7	8.8	15	65%	.426
2018	SYR	AAA	25	3	3	0	13	13	67^1	78	3	2.4	9.4	70	53%	.383
2018	WAS	MLB	25	2	4	0	11	11	50^1	55	8	3.9	8.2	46	54%	.333
2019	HAR	AA	26	2	0	0	5	4	24^2	18	2	1.8	9.9	27	55%	.254
2019	FRE	AAA	26	1	1	0	2	2	10	19	5	3.6	9.0	10	36%	.452
2019	WAS	MLB	26	4	2	0	21	12	78	81	11	3.8	4.7	41	52%	.283
2020	WAS	MLB	27	4	5	0	47	8	82	94	13	3.2	6.0	55	51%	.306

Comparables: Brandon Workman, Daniel Barone, Charles Brewer

The year: 2265. The site: a resurrected Deadspin. An animatronic David Roth reaches into a box of baseball cards, fishing out such notables as Ross, McGowin, Voth, Hellickson and Fedde.

"Hey, let's remember some guys!" he beeps, holding up Fedde's card. "This guy! He threw six pitches. Well, five really. Four, if we're being honest. Look, he definitely throws a sinker, a cutter and a curve."

Across from him, the disembodied head of a staff writer sits in a bubble of isotonic solution adorned with wires delivering enough electrical current to keep it quote-unquote alive. "Interrogative," it displays. "What was his best pitch?"

Roth whirs as if searching for the abbreviated notion of 'best' as it pertains to a Nationals fifth starter and occasional bullpen piece. "Cutter?" he says after a minute.

"Is that an answer or a question?" the staff writer asks.

Roth considers the response, gears visibly turning. "Why not both?" he says, finally. "So is Fedde."

Washington Nationals 2020

YEAR	TEAM	LVL	AGE	WHIP	ERA	DRA	WARP	MPH	FB%	WHF	CSP
2017	HAR	AA	24	1.12	3.04	3.28	1.2				
2017	SYR	AAA	24	1.24	4.76	4.16	0.5				
2017	WAS	MLB	24	2.15	9.39	6.04	-0.1	95.6	61.1	6.7	47.8
2018	SYR	AAA	25	1.43	4.41	5.15	0.3				
2018	WAS	MLB	25	1.53	5.54	4.85	0.3	95.9	54.9	9.5	43.8
2019	HAR	AA	26	0.93	2.55	3.13	0.5				
2019	FRE	AAA	26	2.30	12.60	9.02	-0.2				
2019	WAS	MLB	26	1.46	4.50	6.27	-0.5	94.4	55.2	7.2	46.1
2020	*WAS*	*MLB*	*27*	*1.50*	*5.26*	*5.06*	*0.5*	*94.5*	*56.3*	*8.1*	*46.3*

Erick Fedde, continued

Pitch Shape vs LHH

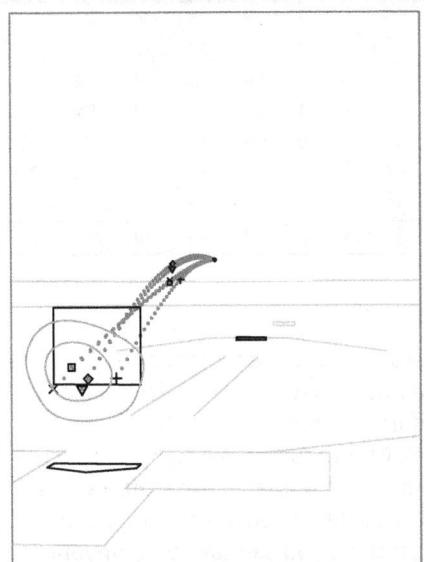

Pitch Shape vs RHH

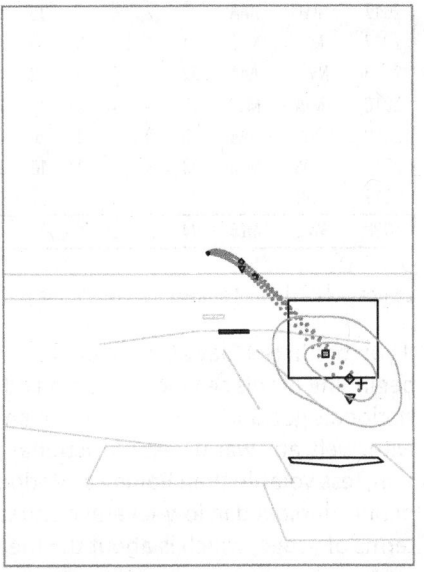

Type	Frequency	Velocity	H Movement	V Movement
● Fastball				
☐ Sinker	54.8%	92.7 [100]	-6.8 [138]	-20.7 [99]
+ Cutter	17.9%	87.5 [93]	4 [113]	-28.5 [84]
▲ Changeup				
✕ Splitter	7.1%	85.7 [103]	-9.8 [93]	-30.5 [95]
▽ Slider	8.0%	80.1 [82]	9.5 [119]	-40.7 [78]
◇ Curveball	11.7%	79.2 [102]	11.4 [116]	-45.3 [105]
⊕ Slow Curveball				
✱ Knuckleball				
▼ Screwball				

Washington Nationals 2020

Javy Guerra RHP
Born: 10/31/85   Age: 34   Bats: R   Throws: R
Height: 6'1"   Weight: 216   Origin: Round 4, 2004 Draft (#118 overall)

YEAR	TEAM	LVL	AGE	W	L	SV	G	GS	IP	H	HR	BB/9	K/9	K	GB%	BABIP
2017	NWO	AAA	31	2	4	2	35	0	51^2	46	7	3.7	7.7	44	42%	.273
2017	MIA	MLB	31	1	1	0	16	0	21	23	2	3.0	5.1	12	52%	.313
2018	NWO	AAA	32	3	0	5	12	0	16^2	9	0	1.6	13.0	24	61%	.273
2018	MIA	MLB	32	1	1	1	32	0	35^2	42	4	3.0	7.6	30	45%	.336
2019	BUF	AAA	33	0	1	1	5	0	7^1	4	0	4.9	7.4	6	28%	.222
2019	WAS	MLB	33	3	1	1	40	0	53^2	55	9	2.0	7.0	42	35%	.279
2019	TOR	MLB	33	0	0	1	11	0	14	12	1	3.2	9.6	15	29%	.297
2020	WAS	MLB	34	2	2	0	33	0	35	36	6	3.0	7.1	28	38%	.292

Comparables: Hector Carrasco, Jay Powell, Joe Smith

If you predicted "Javy Guerra pitches in two (two!) World Series games" at the beginning of this season, congrats and go buy yourself a lottery ticket. The Nationals got Guerra mid-season in an effort to shore up their ailing bullpen with, well, any warm, semi-functional arm. Guerra turned out to be one such arm, less volatile than Rainey or Rodney, but with less-effective stuff. He was mainly deployed in low-leverage situations—a righty version of Matt Grace in terms of usage, which is about the meanest thing you can say about anyone.

YEAR	TEAM	LVL	AGE	WHIP	ERA	DRA	WARP	MPH	FB%	WHF	CSP
2017	NWO	AAA	31	1.30	4.70	4.16	0.6				
2017	MIA	MLB	31	1.43	3.00	5.65	-0.1	94.4	54.9	6	51.7
2018	NWO	AAA	32	0.72	0.00	1.65	0.7				
2018	MIA	MLB	32	1.51	5.55	5.02	0.0	95.3	52.2	9.9	51.5
2019	BUF	AAA	33	1.09	2.45	4.91	0.1				
2019	WAS	MLB	33	1.25	4.86	4.77	0.3	95.5	60	10.3	54.1
2019	TOR	MLB	33	1.21	3.86	6.77	-0.2	95.6	60	8	53.6
2020	WAS	MLB	34	1.37	4.62	4.57	0.3	94.2	56.4	9.3	51.8

Javy Guerra, continued

Pitch Shape vs LHH

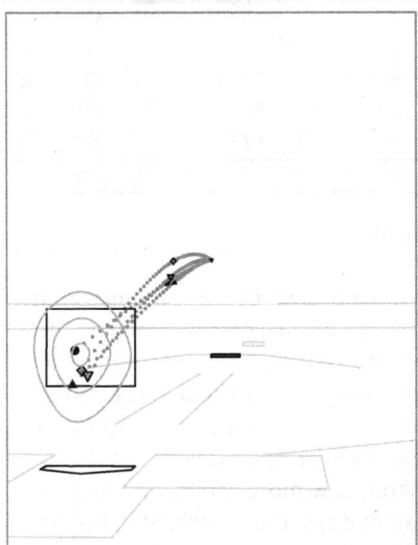

Pitch Shape vs RHH

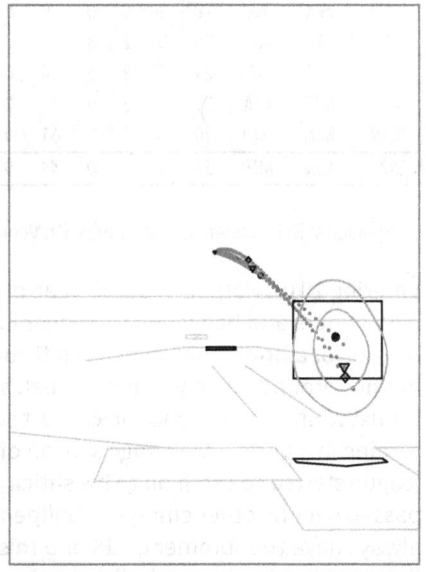

Type	Frequency	Velocity	H Movement	V Movement
● Fastball	59.2%	93 [102]	-3.7 [114]	-12.1 [110]
□ Sinker				
+ Cutter				
▲ Changeup	8.6%	83.7 [94]	-7.6 [116]	-24 [110]
× Splitter				
▽ Slider	23.7%	85.5 [105]	4 [96]	-30.3 [108]
◇ Curveball	8.1%	79.6 [103]	4.7 [89]	-45.6 [104]
✦ Slow Curveball				
✳ Knuckleball				
▼ Screwball				

Nationals Player Analysis - 61

Ryne Harper RHP

Born: 03/27/89   Age: 31   Bats: R   Throws: R
Height: 6'3"   Weight: 215   Origin: Round 37, 2011 Draft (#1136 overall)

YEAR	TEAM	LVL	AGE	W	L	SV	G	GS	IP	H	HR	BB/9	K/9	K	GB%	BABIP
2017	ARK	AA	28	1	0	0	4	0	7^1	2	0	0.0	12.3	10	50%	.143
2017	TAC	AAA	28	3	2	3	37	0	46^1	42	5	4.1	8.7	45	48%	.296
2018	CHT	AA	29	1	2	6	24	0	39	35	0	1.2	11.8	51	40%	.361
2018	ROC	AAA	29	0	3	0	14	0	26	26	2	1.7	12.1	35	62%	.364
2019	MIN	MLB	30	4	2	1	61	0	54^1	54	7	1.7	8.3	50	39%	.301
2020	MIN	MLB	31	2	2	0	44	0	46	45	7	2.3	7.8	40	42%	.289

Comparables: Rob Wooten, Colton Murray, Pat Venditte

Entering 2019, Harper was a 30-year-old who'd thrown over 350 innings in the high minors and had failed to appear in a single Annual despite reaching the majors for a brief promotion. He'd thrown well enough in the high minors to bounce around and earn some sweet, sweet projection-system love for his robust whiff-to-walk tendencies. Last season, he made good on his opportunity, turning in a perfectly average season of big-league middle relief. Sure, the league started to catch on to his shtick as they saw more of him, and he got passed over by other emergent bullpen talent down the stretch. Still, Harper will always have the summer of '19 and this Annual comment to hold onto, if not a firm spot in a big-league bullpen.

YEAR	TEAM	LVL	AGE	WHIP	ERA	DRA	WARP	MPH	FB%	WHF	CSP
2017	ARK	AA	28	0.27	0.00	1.76	0.3				
2017	TAC	AAA	28	1.36	3.88	4.06	0.6				
2018	CHT	AA	29	1.03	2.54	3.19	0.8				
2018	ROC	AAA	29	1.19	5.19	3.34	0.5				
2019	MIN	MLB	30	1.18	3.81	4.67	0.4	91.3	38.7	11.4	52.1
2020	MIN	MLB	31	1.23	3.99	4.11	0.5	90.5	38.5	11.3	51.7

Ryne Harper, continued

Pitch Shape vs LHH

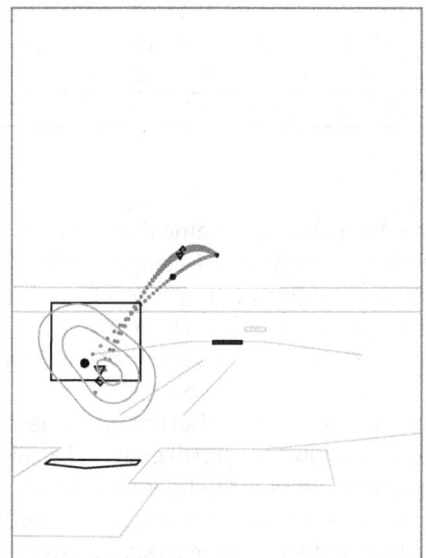

Pitch Shape vs RHH

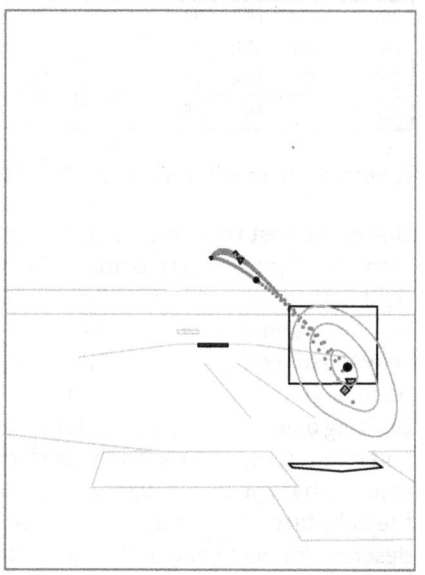

Type	Frequency	Velocity	H Movement	V Movement
● Fastball	38.7%	89.8 [92]	0.5 [132]	-22 [84]
☐ Sinker				
+ Cutter				
▲ Changeup				
✕ Splitter				
▽ Slider	45.2%	75.9 [64]	11.4 [127]	-48.5 [55]
◇ Curveball	15.1%	70.1 [72]	12.4 [120]	-60.6 [72]
✥ Slow Curveball				
✱ Knuckleball				
▼ Screwball				

Washington Nationals 2020

Will Harris   RHP
Born: 08/28/84   Age: 35   Bats: R   Throws: R
Height: 6'4"   Weight: 240   Origin: Round 9, 2006 Draft (#258 overall)

YEAR	TEAM	LVL	AGE	W	L	SV	G	GS	IP	H	HR	BB/9	K/9	K	GB%	BABIP
2017	HOU	MLB	32	3	2	2	46	0	45^1	37	7	1.4	10.3	52	49%	.270
2018	HOU	MLB	33	5	3	0	61	0	56^2	48	3	2.2	10.2	64	54%	.306
2019	HOU	MLB	34	4	1	4	68	0	60	42	6	2.1	9.3	62	54%	.245
2020	WAS	MLB	35	2	2	0	33	0	35	31	4	2.8	9.7	38	51%	.291

Comparables: Heath Bell, Fernando Salas, Mark Melancon

One of the best kept secrets of the Astros rebuild, it was a shame that the last memory Harris has in Houston is the ball that Howie Kendrick clanged off the right field foul pole in Game 7 of the World Series—though they'll now be able to reminisce about it over the post-game spread in Washington. The Astros selected him off of waivers when the Diamondbacks couldn't find room for him on their 40-man roster. All he's done since is sport a 2.36 ERA over 297 innings. Utilizing a two-pitch mix of cutter and curveball has been lethal to both lefties and righties, making Harris the perfect combination of high strikeout and weak contact that you would want in any arm trotting out of the bullpen. Maybe it's the baby face or the relatively low velocity, but he's never gotten the credit he deserves for being one of the more consistent bullpen arms in the game over the past few years.

YEAR	TEAM	LVL	AGE	WHIP	ERA	DRA	WARP	MPH	FB%	WHF	CSP
2017	HOU	MLB	32	0.97	2.98	2.45	1.4	93.6	68.7	13.9	46.9
2018	HOU	MLB	33	1.09	3.49	2.32	1.7	94.0	62.3	14.5	42.5
2019	HOU	MLB	34	0.93	1.50	3.45	1.2	93.0	58	12.6	45.2
2020	WAS	MLB	35	1.19	3.29	3.37	0.8	92.3	60.5	13.3	43.9

Will Harris, continued

Pitch Shape vs LHH

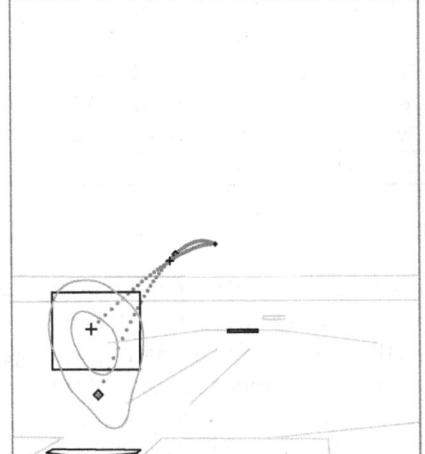

Pitch Shape vs RHH

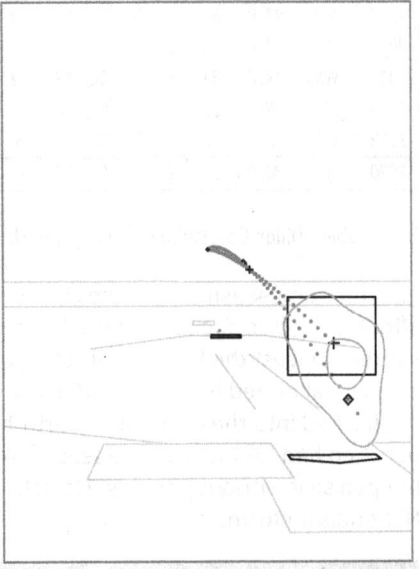

Type	Frequency	Velocity	H Movement	V Movement
● Fastball				
☐ Sinker				
+ Cutter	58.0%	91.5 [118]	3.6 [111]	-19.5 [117]
▲ Changeup				
✕ Splitter				
▽ Slider				
◇ Curveball	42.0%	81.5 [110]	10.8 [113]	-50.5 [94]
⊕ Slow Curveball				
✱ Knuckleball				
▼ Screwball				

Jeremy Hellickson RHP

Born: 04/08/87   Age: 33   Bats: R   Throws: R
Height: 6'1"   Weight: 190   Origin: Round 4, 2005 Draft (#118 overall)

YEAR	TEAM	LVL	AGE	W	L	SV	G	GS	IP	H	HR	BB/9	K/9	K	GB%	BABIP
2017	PHI	MLB	30	6	5	0	20	20	112^1	111	22	2.4	5.2	65	37%	.255
2017	BAL	MLB	30	2	6	0	10	10	51^2	49	13	3.0	5.4	31	36%	.225
2018	WAS	MLB	31	5	3	0	19	19	91^1	78	11	2.0	6.4	65	47%	.252
2019	NAT	RK	32	1	1	0	5	4	16^2	11	1	1.1	11.9	22	49%	.250
2019	WAS	MLB	32	2	3	0	9	8	39	47	9	4.6	6.9	30	39%	.309
2020	WAS	MLB	33	2	2	0	33	0	35	40	9	3.0	6.7	26	41%	.288

Comparables: Dillon Gee, Pedro Astacio, Clay Buchholz

The third time wasn't quite the charm. Hellickson returned to the Nationals after testing free agency in 2019, having previously been a reliable-ish fifth starter—at least the first two times through the order, before his batting average against ballooned to north of .400. In his return, the former AL Rookie of the Year diminished into the Nationals' fourth-best fifth starter before shoulder stiffness benched him for much of the season. After spending September warming a bullpen seat without pitching, Hellickson is unlikely to see another season in a Nationals uniform.

YEAR	TEAM	LVL	AGE	WHIP	ERA	DRA	WARP	MPH	FB%	WHF	CSP
2017	PHI	MLB	30	1.26	4.73	5.99	-0.5	91.6	54.3	9.1	45.6
2017	BAL	MLB	30	1.28	6.97	6.97	-0.8	92.0	54.3	8.5	43.9
2018	WAS	MLB	31	1.07	3.45	4.19	1.2	91.8	51.4	9	48.5
2019	NAT	RK	32	0.78	2.16	0.55	1.0				
2019	WAS	MLB	32	1.72	6.23	6.84	-0.5	90.8	61.2	6.7	46.4
2020	WAS	MLB	33	1.47	6.04	6.01	-0.2	90.6	54.1	8.4	46.2

Jeremy Hellickson, continued

Pitch Shape vs LHH

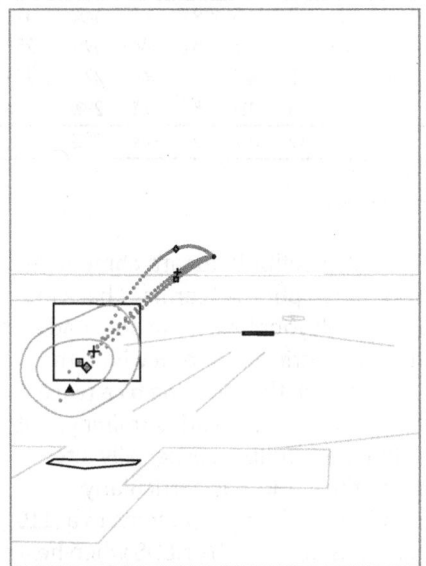

Pitch Shape vs RHH

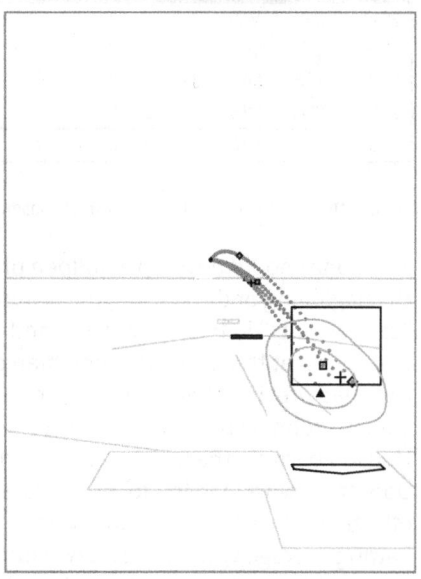

Type	Frequency	Velocity	H Movement	V Movement
● Fastball	5.8%	89.3 [91]	-11.1 [81]	-17.4 [96]
□ Sinker	37.3%	89.3 [83]	-13.3 [96]	-21 [98]
+ Cutter	18.1%	86.2 [84]	-0.7 [85]	-21.1 [111]
▲ Changeup	25.5%	80.4 [82]	-7.2 [118]	-29.5 [94]
✕ Splitter				
▽ Slider				
◇ Curveball	13.3%	74.2 [85]	10.8 [113]	-57.4 [79]
⊕ Slow Curveball				
✱ Knuckleball				
▼ Screwball				

Daniel Hudson RHP

Born: 03/09/87 Age: 33 Bats: R Throws: R
Height: 6'3" Weight: 225 Origin: Round 5, 2008 Draft (#150 overall)

YEAR	TEAM	LVL	AGE	W	L	SV	G	GS	IP	H	HR	BB/9	K/9	K	GB%	BABIP
2017	PIT	MLB	30	2	7	0	71	0	61^2	57	7	4.8	9.6	66	44%	.312
2018	LAN	MLB	31	3	2	0	40	1	46	38	6	3.5	8.6	44	39%	.256
2019	TOR	MLB	32	6	3	2	45	1	48	38	5	4.3	9.0	48	42%	.258
2019	WAS	MLB	32	3	0	6	24	0	25	18	3	1.4	8.3	23	29%	.227
2020	WAS	MLB	33	2	2	0	44	0	47	44	7	3.7	9.3	49	39%	.292

Comparables: Wade Davis, Andrew Cashner, Jason Isringhausen

Someone should develop a bullpen phone with a defibrillator attachment. At the beginning of the season, the Nationals bullpen put the "cardiac" back in "cardiac Nats" in that they would and could break your heart. Hudson made less of a splash at the trade deadline than did Hunter Strickland, with whom the Nats had previous bad blood, an attempt to staunch the bleeding by a twice Tommy John'd starter-turned-reliever cut by the Angels in spring training. But Hudson became the beating heart of the Nationals bullpen, especially after Doolittle's workload led to an August stint on the IL. He was particularly effective in heart-palpitation-inducing situations, holding opponents to a .119 batting average with RISP and two outs, like in Game 2 of the NLDS when he punched Corey Seager out on a heartburn-generating, bases-loaded swinging strike. There are questions as to the sustainability of his efforts, notably the gap between his ERA and DRA, but as Damn Yankees reminds us, sometimes you just gotta have heart.

YEAR	TEAM	LVL	AGE	WHIP	ERA	DRA	WARP	MPH	FB%	WHF	CSP
2017	PIT	MLB	30	1.46	4.38	4.74	0.3	97.1	60.2	12.8	47.3
2018	LAN	MLB	31	1.22	4.11	4.63	0.2	97.1	54.4	14	51.3
2019	TOR	MLB	32	1.27	3.00	5.10	0.1	97.5	70.2	11.1	47.5
2019	WAS	MLB	32	0.88	1.44	3.82	0.4	97.8	72.4	12	54.4
2020	WAS	MLB	33	1.34	4.34	4.28	0.6	96.3	63.4	12.2	49

Daniel Hudson, continued

Pitch Shape vs LHH   *Pitch Shape vs RHH*

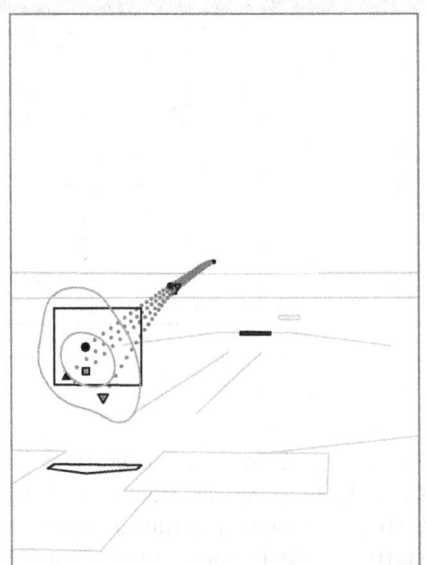
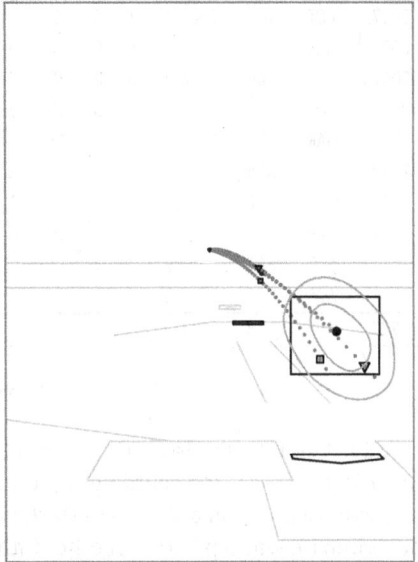

Type	Frequency	Velocity	H Movement	V Movement
● Fastball	64.0%	96.5 [112]	-7.4 [97]	-12.8 [108]
▢ Sinker	6.9%	95.9 [117]	-14.3 [89]	-17.8 [109]
+ Cutter				
▲ Changeup	5.8%	89 [114]	-15.7 [79]	-21.2 [118]
✕ Splitter				
▽ Slider	23.3%	87 [111]	2.1 [88]	-30.6 [107]
◇ Curveball				
⊕ Slow Curveball				
✸ Knuckleball				
▼ Screwball				

Kyle McGowin RHP

Born: 11/27/91 Age: 28 Bats: R Throws: R
Height: 6'3" Weight: 195 Origin: Round 5, 2013 Draft (#157 overall)

YEAR	TEAM	LVL	AGE	W	L	SV	G	GS	IP	H	HR	BB/9	K/9	K	GB%	BABIP
2017	POT	A+	25	1	1	0	2	2	10	10	1	3.6	8.1	9	41%	.321
2017	HAR	AA	25	1	5	0	8	8	42^2	58	12	3.4	8.2	39	41%	.346
2017	SYR	AAA	25	1	6	0	9	9	45^2	51	3	3.9	5.3	27	52%	.316
2018	POT	A+	26	1	1	0	2	2	11	8	2	2.5	11.5	14	42%	.250
2018	HAR	AA	26	4	3	0	13	13	78	62	7	2.2	10.8	94	50%	.281
2018	SYR	AAA	26	3	2	0	8	8	52^2	26	3	1.5	7.5	44	44%	.177
2018	WAS	MLB	26	0	0	0	5	1	7^2	6	2	5.9	9.4	8	33%	.211
2019	HAR	AA	27	1	1	0	6	6	32^1	22	2	2.5	10.0	36	40%	.263
2019	FRE	AAA	27	7	2	0	11	11	60^2	59	8	2.5	10.1	68	47%	.321
2019	WAS	MLB	27	0	0	1	7	1	16	22	7	2.2	10.1	18	45%	.326
2020	WAS	MLB	28	3	3	0	26	6	53	56	10	3.2	9.5	56	44%	.316

Comparables: Austin Voth, Tyler Beede, Mike Mayers

May 24: A cloudy, rainless Friday night between two teams with the worst records in the NL—the scuffling Nationals and the limp Marlins. No one expected a season to pivot on a McGowin start, not when he gave up five runs on six hits, not when he was a pieced-together fifth-starter on a team that couldn't seem to piece together a win. Not when he was trying to do something as foolish as being a fly-ball pitcher in the juiced-ball, launch-angle era. The Nats won that game through the strange tactic of scoring more runs in the eighth than they surrendered, and McGowin would go on to make a handful of other relief appearances, an unspectacular component of one of baseball's least spectacular bullpens, who happened to be in the right place and time to witness a turnaround.

YEAR	TEAM	LVL	AGE	WHIP	ERA	DRA	WARP	MPH	FB%	WHF	CSP
2017	POT	A+	25	1.40	1.80	4.53	0.1				
2017	HAR	AA	25	1.73	6.54	7.96	-1.4				
2017	SYR	AAA	25	1.55	6.31	5.68	0.0				
2018	POT	A+	26	1.00	4.09	2.96	0.3				
2018	HAR	AA	26	1.04	3.69	2.54	2.5				
2018	SYR	AAA	26	0.66	1.20	2.03	2.1				
2018	WAS	MLB	26	1.43	5.87	4.65	0.0	92.5	59.2	12.3	38.9
2019	HAR	AA	27	0.96	2.51	3.24	0.7				
2019	FRE	AAA	27	1.25	3.86	3.10	2.1				
2019	WAS	MLB	27	1.62	10.12	3.61	0.3	93.3	52.4	13.2	42
2020	WAS	MLB	28	1.40	4.96	4.83	0.5	92.5	54.5	13	40.8

Kyle McGowin, continued

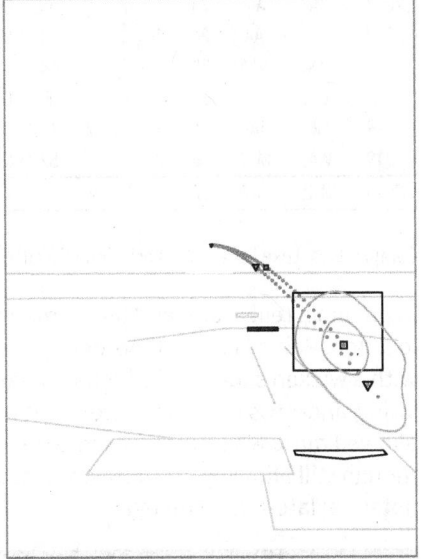

Type	Frequency	Velocity	H Movement	V Movement
● Fastball	3.4%	92 [99]	-7.5 [97]	-14.4 [104]
☐ Sinker	49.0%	91.2 [93]	-13.1 [97]	-20.4 [100]
+ Cutter				
▲ Changeup				
✕ Splitter				
▽ Slider	44.6%	83.6 [96]	4.3 [97]	-32.7 [101]
◇ Curveball				
⊕ Slow Curveball				
✱ Knuckleball				
▼ Screwball				

Tanner Rainey   RHP

Born: 12/25/92   Age: 27   Bats: R   Throws: R
Height: 6'2"   Weight: 235   Origin: Round 2, 2015 Draft (#71 overall)

YEAR	TEAM	LVL	AGE	W	L	SV	G	GS	IP	H	HR	BB/9	K/9	K	GB%	BABIP
2017	DAY	A+	24	2	2	9	39	0	45	21	4	4.4	15.4	77	47%	.230
2017	PEN	AA	24	1	1	4	14	0	17	8	2	5.8	14.3	27	62%	.222
2018	LOU	AAA	25	7	2	3	44	0	51	25	2	6.2	11.5	65	37%	.221
2018	CIN	MLB	25	0	0	0	8	0	7	13	4	15.4	9.0	7	31%	.409
2019	FRE	AAA	26	2	2	2	16	0	18	16	1	6.0	16.0	32	57%	.417
2019	WAS	MLB	26	2	3	0	52	0	48^1	32	6	7.1	13.8	74	54%	.283
2020	WAS	MLB	27	3	2	4	49	0	52	41	6	6.2	14.2	82	47%	.327

Comparables: Luke Farrell, Vic Black, Cody Carroll

In pitching, real estate and life, sometimes all that matters is location, location, location. Rainey has stuff bordering on unfair—a fastball in the high-90s paired with a wicked slider in the high-80s—and he generated an incredible 41 percent swing-and-miss rate this season. But his issue was and is locating pitches. He allowed more walks than hits in 2019, cutting his previous season's WHIP in half, though still allowing for more on-base traffic than one would want from a potential late-inning reliever.

YEAR	TEAM	LVL	AGE	WHIP	ERA	DRA	WARP	MPH	FB%	WHF	CSP
2017	DAY	A+	24	0.96	3.80	1.74	1.7				
2017	PEN	AA	24	1.12	1.59	3.18	0.3				
2018	LOU	AAA	25	1.18	2.65	3.08	1.2				
2018	CIN	MLB	25	3.57	24.43	9.00	-0.3	100.1	71.4	12.2	38.9
2019	FRE	AAA	26	1.56	4.00	2.63	0.6				
2019	WAS	MLB	26	1.45	3.91	3.07	1.2	99.5	70.8	18.8	43.7
2020	WAS	MLB	27	1.48	4.29	4.11	0.7	99.1	71.7	18	42.1

Tanner Rainey, continued

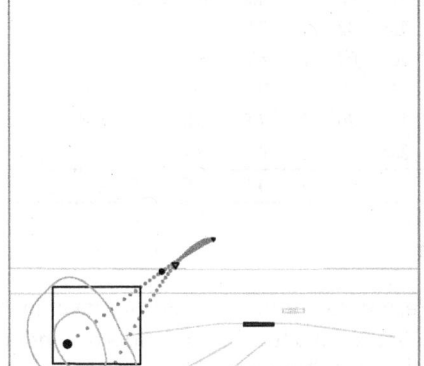
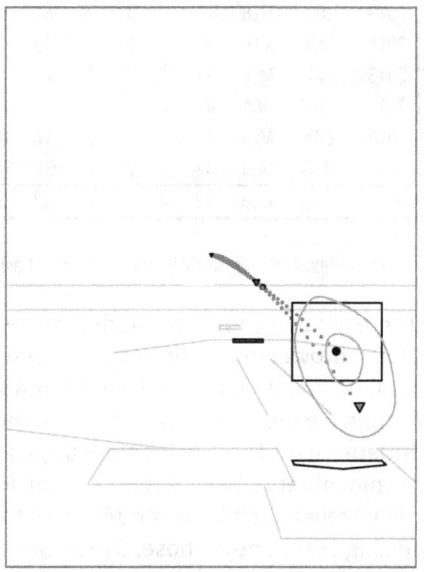

Type	Frequency	Velocity	H Movement	V Movement
● Fastball	70.8%	98 [116]	-3.3 [116]	-9.7 [116]
☐ Sinker				
+ Cutter				
▲ Changeup				
✕ Splitter				
▽ Slider	29.0%	87.5 [113]	4.3 [97]	-34.1 [97]
◇ Curveball				
⊕ Slow Curveball				
✳ Knuckleball				
▼ Screwball				

Fernando Rodney RHP

Born: 03/18/77   Age: 43   Bats: R   Throws: R
Height: 5'11"   Weight: 240   Origin: International Free Agent, 1997

YEAR	TEAM	LVL	AGE	W	L	SV	G	GS	IP	H	HR	BB/9	K/9	K	GB%	BABIP
2017	ARI	MLB	40	5	4	39	61	0	55^1	40	3	4.2	10.6	65	54%	.274
2018	MIN	MLB	41	3	2	25	46	0	43^2	42	5	3.9	10.3	50	45%	.319
2018	OAK	MLB	41	1	1	0	22	0	20^2	20	2	5.7	8.7	20	46%	.316
2019	FRE	AAA	42	0	2	0	9	0	8	8	1	10.1	12.4	11	50%	.333
2019	OAK	MLB	42	0	2	0	17	0	14^1	20	2	7.5	8.8	14	55%	.429
2019	WAS	MLB	42	0	3	2	38	0	33^1	29	3	4.3	9.4	35	48%	.302
2020	WAS	MLB	43	2	2	0	33	0	35	32	4	4.5	9.8	38	48%	.302

Comparables: Al Reyes, Rudy Seanez, Santiago Casilla

There are two Fernandos Rodney: One, Fernando Rodney, the oldest player in MLB. Thrower of a truly nasty changeup. Wearer of a terrific hat, and a reminder that, no matter your age, baseball is a kid's game. That despite everything, this is supposed to be *fun*. The other, Rodney Fernando, the oldest player in MLB. Hittable, over-the-hill, his glory days well behind him, a flat changeup and an imminent retirement. A relic, a fossil. Rodney has thrown more pitches than any active relief pitcher—some 16,500 of them since 2002. Some days, it seems he's feeling every one of those. Others are a reminder that there's value in youthful enthusiasm and that there's value in age and treachery. And that baseball should be wide enough to contain both.

YEAR	TEAM	LVL	AGE	WHIP	ERA	DRA	WARP	MPH	FB%	WHF	CSP
2017	ARI	MLB	40	1.19	4.23	3.63	1.0	96.9	59.5	13.2	45.4
2018	MIN	MLB	41	1.40	3.09	3.85	0.5	97.0	71.8	13.1	46.8
2018	OAK	MLB	41	1.60	3.92	4.52	0.1	97.1	68.7	9.5	43.9
2019	FRE	AAA	42	2.12	4.50	4.73	0.1				
2019	OAK	MLB	42	2.23	9.42	5.36	0.0	95.4	64.6	9.1	43.1
2019	WAS	MLB	42	1.35	4.05	4.32	0.4	96.7	69.4	13.2	45.7
2020	WAS	MLB	43	1.43	4.30	4.39	0.4	94.7	64.2	11.7	43.4

Fernando Rodney, continued

Pitch Shape vs LHH

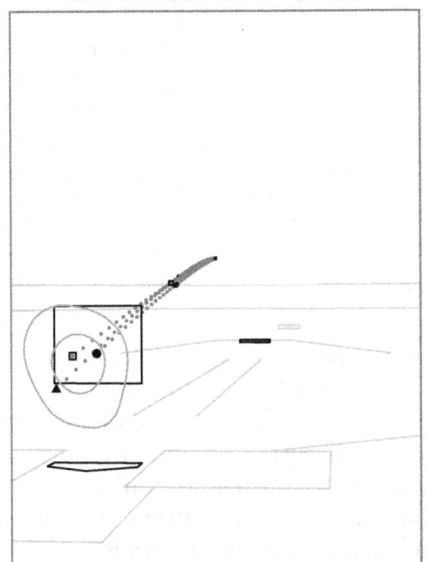

Pitch Shape vs RHH

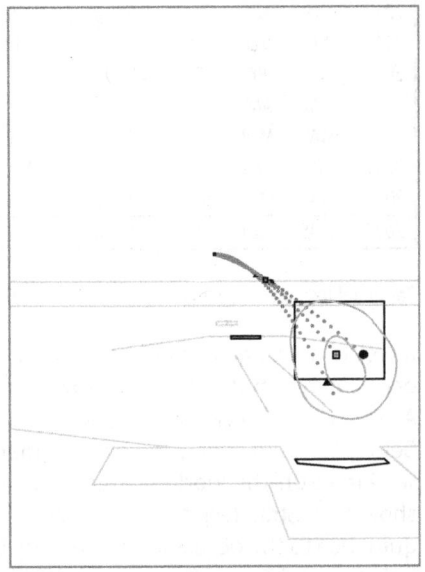

Type	Frequency	Velocity	H Movement	V Movement
● Fastball	20.6%	94.7 [106]	-4.5 [110]	-12.2 [110]
☐ Sinker	47.4%	93.8 [106]	-11.5 [107]	-16.7 [113]
+ Cutter				
▲ Changeup	28.7%	83.3 [93]	-12.9 [92]	-28.7 [96]
✕ Splitter				
▽ Slider	3.3%	86.6 [109]	2.4 [89]	-26 [121]
◇ Curveball				
✥ Slow Curveball				
✳ Knuckleball				
▼ Screwball				

Washington Nationals 2020

Joe Ross RHP
Born: 05/21/93   Age: 27   Bats: R   Throws: R
Height: 6'4"   Weight: 220   Origin: Round 1, 2011 Draft (#25 overall)

YEAR	TEAM	LVL	AGE	W	L	SV	G	GS	IP	H	HR	BB/9	K/9	K	GB%	BABIP
2017	SYR	AAA	24	2	2	0	5	5	27^2	33	3	2.6	7.2	22	37%	.341
2017	WAS	MLB	24	5	3	0	13	13	73^2	88	16	2.4	8.3	68	41%	.332
2018	NAT	RK	25	0	0	0	2	2	6	0	0	4.5	12.0	8	56%	.000
2018	SYR	AAA	25	2	0	0	2	2	11^2	12	0	3.1	3.1	4	43%	.273
2018	WAS	MLB	25	0	2	0	3	3	16	17	3	2.2	3.9	7	36%	.269
2019	FRE	AAA	26	2	3	0	8	8	40	48	2	1.8	7.2	32	50%	.368
2019	WAS	MLB	26	4	4	0	27	9	64	74	7	4.6	8.0	57	45%	.345
2020	WAS	MLB	27	6	6	0	36	16	102	104	16	3.3	8.0	90	45%	.300

Comparables: Kevin Gausman, A.J. Cole, Alex Cobb

It would have been an epic story. Ross, coming back from Tommy John, occasional fifth starter and unspectacular long man, takes on the Houston Astros when a neck injury felled the mighty Max Scherzer in Game 5 of the World Series. It would have been epic, Homeric, an unlikely rise-from-the-ashes, workman-on-the-world's-largest-stage story, if only the Nationals' offense had shown up. Still, despite pitching well against baseball's best offense, Ross didn't quite rise to the occasion. His velocity has risen, though, his ground-ball-inducing sinker and four-seamer back up to their pre-surgery speeds, along with reworked, slurvier slider, all indications he'll return this year as a protagonist and not just a footnote.

YEAR	TEAM	LVL	AGE	WHIP	ERA	DRA	WARP	MPH	FB%	WHF	CSP
2017	SYR	AAA	24	1.48	4.88	6.15	-0.1				
2017	WAS	MLB	24	1.47	5.01	4.19	1.1	94.1	54.8	11	48.9
2018	NAT	RK	25	0.50	0.00	1.05	0.3				
2018	SYR	AAA	25	1.37	3.09	5.87	0.0				
2018	WAS	MLB	25	1.31	5.06	7.08	-0.3	94.9	56	9.2	44.9
2019	FRE	AAA	26	1.40	4.28	4.67	0.8				
2019	WAS	MLB	26	1.67	5.48	6.38	-0.5	96.0	62.8	11.2	45.3
2020	WAS	MLB	27	1.39	4.63	4.54	1.4	94.7	60.1	11.1	46.6

Joe Ross, continued

Pitch Shape vs LHH

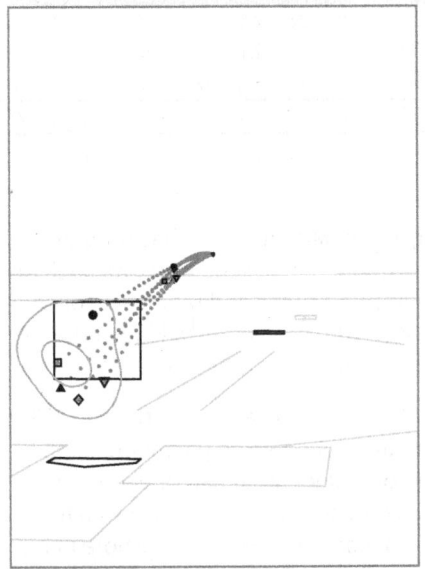

Pitch Shape vs RHH

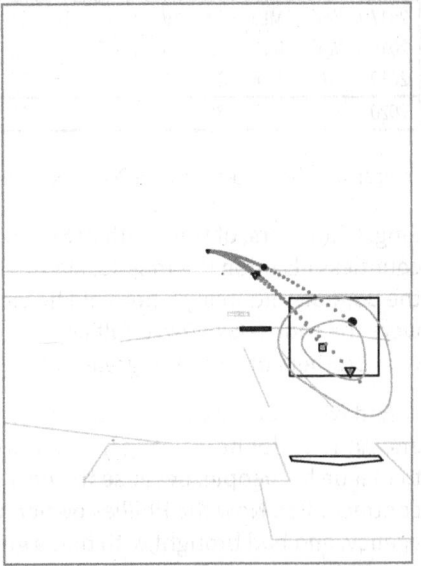

Type	Frequency	Velocity	H Movement	V Movement
● Fastball	23.8%	94.5 [106]	-6.3 [102]	-14.5 [104]
□ Sinker	39.0%	94.2 [108]	-12.5 [101]	-18.4 [107]
+ Cutter				
▲ Changeup	7.6%	88.3 [111]	-12.6 [93]	-24.2 [109]
✕ Splitter				
▽ Slider	20.7%	88.3 [116]	2.2 [88]	-26.3 [120]
◇ Curveball	8.9%	81.3 [109]	1.8 [77]	-40.5 [115]
✪ Slow Curveball				
✱ Knuckleball				
▼ Screwball				

Washington Nationals 2020

Max Scherzer   RHP
Born: 07/27/84   Age: 35   Bats: R   Throws: R
Height: 6'3"   Weight: 215   Origin: Round 1, 2006 Draft (#11 overall)

YEAR	TEAM	LVL	AGE	W	L	SV	G	GS	IP	H	HR	BB/9	K/9	K	GB%	BABIP
2017	WAS	MLB	32	16	6	0	31	31	200^2	126	22	2.5	12.0	268	38%	.245
2018	WAS	MLB	33	18	7	0	33	33	220^2	150	23	2.1	12.2	300	35%	.265
2019	WAS	MLB	34	11	7	0	27	27	172^1	144	18	1.7	12.7	243	41%	.322
2020	WAS	MLB	35	13	8	0	29	29	187	147	25	2.3	12.5	255	39%	.297

Comparables: Tim Lincecum, David Price, Pedro Martinez

Sing, Oh Writers, of the Wrath of Scherzer, Son of Missouri, that has brought countless ills upon the majors. Many a brave soul did he send hurrying back to the dugout, and many a hero did he yield as prey to yips and reporters, for so were the counsels of Rizzo fulfilled the day on which Bryce, new king of the city with brothers of love, and great Scherzer, fell out with one another.

And which of the owners was it that set them to quarrel? It was the son of Ted and Annette, for he was angry with Harper, and set deferred payments upon him to plague his people, because the new son of Philadelphia had dishonored his contract offer. Now the Phillies owner had come to the offices of Boras in free agency, and had brought with him a great ransom. Moreover, Bryce bore in his hands the slugger of Louisville, wreathed in pine tar, and he beset the Nationals but most of all Scherzer and Strasburg, who were their aces.

"Sons of Washington," Scherzer cried. "And all other Nationals. May the baseball gods who dwell in Cooperstown grant you strength to sack the City of the Liberty Bell. And that you reach home plate in safety. But earn me the Curly W, and offer run support, in reverence to Cy Young, father of pitcher wins."

YEAR	TEAM	LVL	AGE	WHIP	ERA	DRA	WARP	MPH	FB%	WHF	CSP
2017	WAS	MLB	32	0.90	2.51	2.32	7.3	96.2	48.7	16.7	48.7
2018	WAS	MLB	33	0.91	2.53	2.29	7.7	96.6	50.1	17.3	50
2019	WAS	MLB	34	1.03	2.92	2.48	6.2	97.1	48.3	17.8	49.2
2020	WAS	MLB	35	1.04	2.71	2.90	6.0	95.4	48.2	17	48.5

Max Scherzer, continued

Pitch Shape vs LHH	Pitch Shape vs RHH
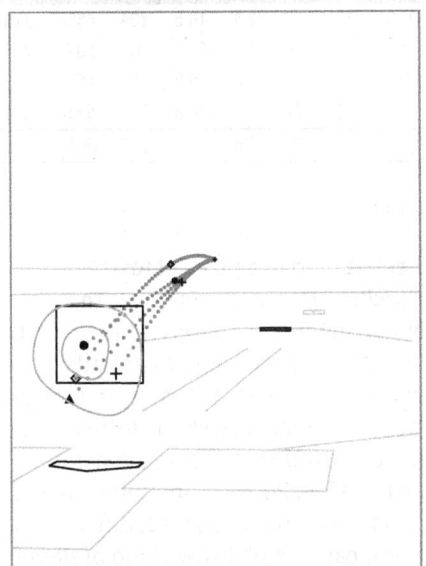	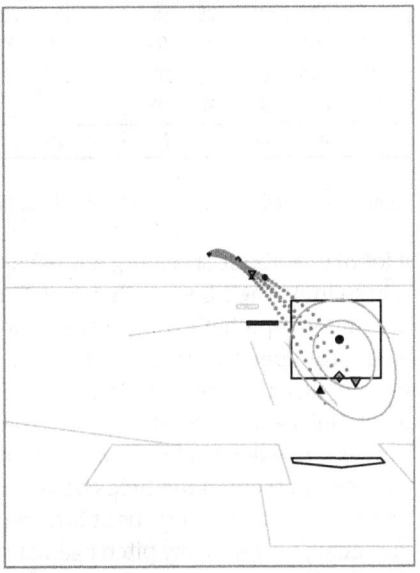

Type	Frequency	Velocity	H Movement	V Movement
● Fastball	48.3%	95.3 [108]	-10.3 [85]	-14.6 [103]
☐ Sinker				
+ Cutter	8.1%	90.1 [109]	-0.2 [88]	-23.1 [104]
▲ Changeup	14.5%	84.7 [98]	-13.4 [90]	-31.9 [87]
✕ Splitter				
▽ Slider	20.4%	85.9 [107]	3.2 [93]	-31.6 [104]
◇ Curveball	8.7%	78.9 [101]	9.7 [109]	-44.3 [107]
⊕ Slow Curveball				
✻ Knuckleball				
▼ Screwball				

Stephen Strasburg RHP

Born: 07/20/88 Age: 31 Bats: R Throws: R
Height: 6'5" Weight: 235 Origin: Round 1, 2009 Draft (#1 overall)

YEAR	TEAM	LVL	AGE	W	L	SV	G	GS	IP	H	HR	BB/9	K/9	K	GB%	BABIP
2017	WAS	MLB	28	15	4	0	28	28	175^1	131	13	2.4	10.5	204	48%	.274
2018	POT	A+	29	0	1	0	2	2	9	7	1	1.0	12.0	12	50%	.261
2018	WAS	MLB	29	10	7	0	22	22	130	118	18	2.6	10.8	156	45%	.309
2019	WAS	MLB	30	18	6	0	33	33	209	161	24	2.4	10.8	251	52%	.274
2020	WAS	MLB	31	12	9	0	29	29	178	154	23	2.6	10.9	216	50%	.300

Comparables: Pedro Martinez, Clayton Kershaw, Jake Peavy

A lot of talk about Strasburg has always been rooted in a place of toxic masculinity—he's been called "soft,", an "orchid." But he's a reminder that some orchids are epiphytic; they thrive best high up in the tree canopy, able to extract water from periodic rainfall, roots going from desiccated white to a sudden photosynthetic green under favorable environmental conditions. If Strasburg is an orchid, he's that kind. Gone are the days of the blazing fastball. Instead, he thrives on mixing his four-seamer with that devastating changeup, generating whiffs 45 percent of the times batters dare to swing. Perhaps unappreciated (if one could call anything about Strasburg's pitching unappreciated) is his curveball, his put-away pitch against righties, capable of its own kind of slow devastation—a reminder that it's often not the fastest, but the most adaptable, who are able to survive.

YEAR	TEAM	LVL	AGE	WHIP	ERA	DRA	WARP	MPH	FB%	WHF	CSP
2017	WAS	MLB	28	1.02	2.52	2.93	5.2	97.8	51.9	13.8	49.3
2018	POT	A+	29	0.89	1.00	2.56	0.3				
2018	WAS	MLB	29	1.20	3.74	2.97	3.5	97.5	52	13	47.2
2019	WAS	MLB	30	1.04	3.32	2.13	8.3	95.8	48.3	14.4	44.6
2020	WAS	MLB	31	1.16	3.24	3.34	4.9	95.9	49.8	13.8	46.3

Stephen Strasburg, continued

Pitch Shape vs LHH

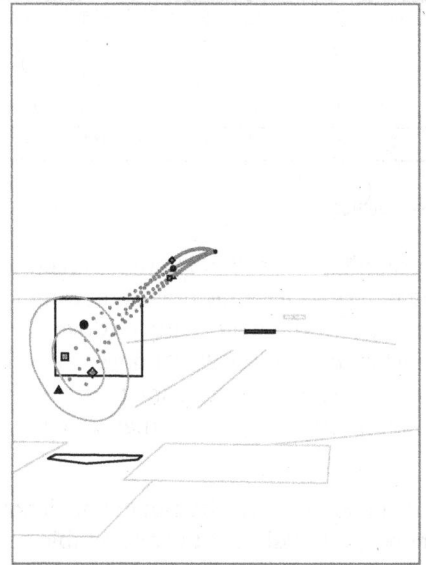

Pitch Shape vs RHH

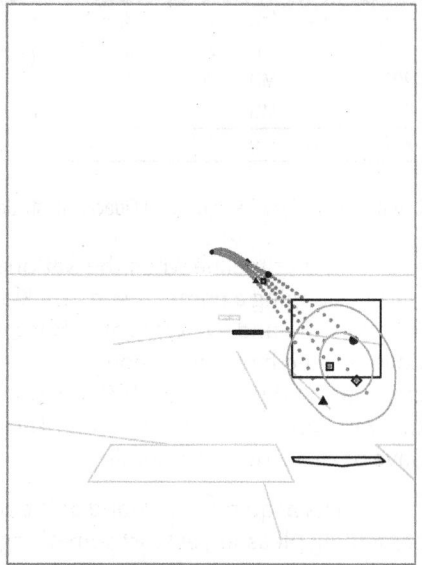

Type	Frequency	Velocity	H Movement	V Movement
● Fastball	29.8%	94.4 [106]	-8.5 [93]	-14.3 [104]
☐ Sinker	18.5%	94.1 [108]	-14.2 [90]	-18.5 [106]
+ Cutter				
▲ Changeup	20.7%	88.2 [110]	-13.7 [88]	-29.2 [95]
✕ Splitter				
▽ Slider				
◇ Curveball	30.6%	81.5 [110]	11.9 [118]	-44.1 [107]
⊕ Slow Curveball				
✳ Knuckleball				
▼ Screwball				

Hunter Strickland   RHP

Born: 09/24/88   Age: 31   Bats: R   Throws: R
Height: 6'3"   Weight: 225   Origin: Round 18, 2007 Draft (#564 overall)

YEAR	TEAM	LVL	AGE	W	L	SV	G	GS	IP	H	HR	BB/9	K/9	K	GB%	BABIP
2017	SFN	MLB	28	4	3	1	68	0	61^1	59	4	4.3	8.5	58	38%	.314
2018	SFN	MLB	29	3	5	14	49	0	45^1	43	5	4.2	7.3	37	40%	.277
2019	SEA	MLB	30	0	1	2	4	0	3^1	2	1	0.0	8.1	3	33%	.125
2019	WAS	MLB	30	2	0	0	24	0	21	20	5	3.4	6.4	15	33%	.242
2020	WAS	MLB	31	2	2	0	39	0	42	38	6	3.2	8.2	38	36%	.274

Comparables: Blake Treinen, Kevin Quackenbush, Jeremy Jeffress

In a different timeline when the Nationals didn't win the World Series, Bryce Harper slapping a home run off Strickland two years after the brawl following a hit-by-pitch—and five years after Harper put a Strickland pitch into McCovey Cove—would have been enough #narrative for anyone. The 2019 home run came late in the game in which the Nationals clinched a postseason berth, one the Nats won 6-5 buoyed by a Trea Turner grand slam, a footnote that would have been a lede any other time.

    The Nats acquired Strickland at the trade deadline in an attempt to find, if not something pleasant, at least something new, given their worst of all possible bullpens in the first half of the season. It was a move many decried not because of the pitch that hit Harper, but because of the downstream effects on fan-favorite former-National and now-former-Giant Michael Morse. Strickland did, in fact, become a member of the Nats bullpen, in all the damning ways that means, and it became evident that his habit of surrendering homers wasn't special to Harper but a symptom of broader concerns about injury recovery.

YEAR	TEAM	LVL	AGE	WHIP	ERA	DRA	WARP	MPH	FB%	WHF	CSP
2017	SFN	MLB	28	1.43	2.64	5.11	0.0	97.9	68.5	11.7	49.2
2018	SFN	MLB	29	1.41	3.97	4.49	0.2	97.5	64.3	11.8	46.9
2019	SEA	MLB	30	0.60	8.10	6.19	0.0	97.0	65.8	9.5	39.8
2019	WAS	MLB	30	1.33	5.14	6.72	-0.3	98.1	65.8	12.4	48.5
2020	WAS	MLB	31	1.26	3.93	3.97	0.7	96.9	65.8	11.8	47.7

Hunter Strickland, continued

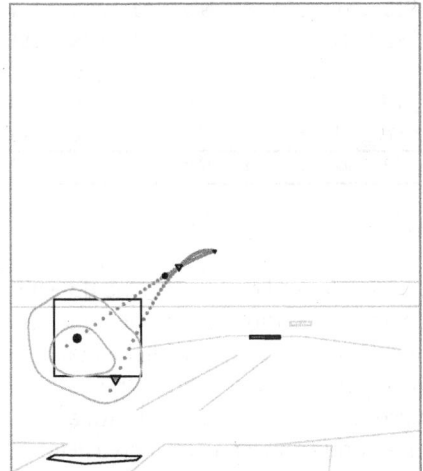
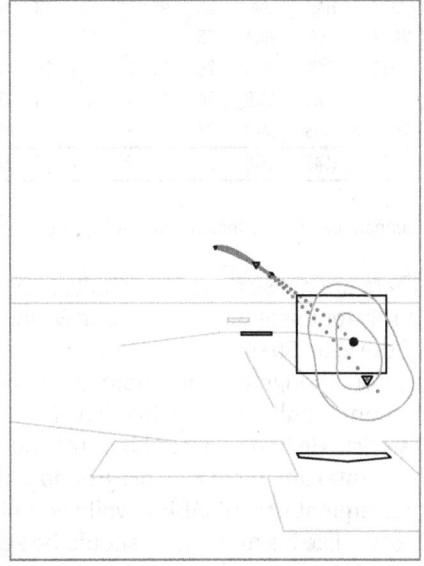

Type	Frequency	Velocity	H Movement	V Movement
● Fastball	58.0%	96.1 [111]	-5.1 [108]	-13.1 [107]
□ Sinker	7.6%	95.5 [115]	-11.7 [106]	-16.5 [114]
+ Cutter				
▲ Changeup	4.1%	89.6 [116]	-11.7 [97]	-21.3 [118]
✕ Splitter				
▽ Slider	29.8%	83.7 [97]	8.4 [114]	-36.5 [90]
◇ Curveball				
⊕ Slow Curveball				
✷ Knuckleball				
▼ Screwball				

Wander Suero RHP

Born: 09/15/91   Age: 28   Bats: R   Throws: R
Height: 6'4"   Weight: 211   Origin: International Free Agent, 2010

YEAR	TEAM	LVL	AGE	W	L	SV	G	GS	IP	H	HR	BB/9	K/9	K	GB%	BABIP
2017	HAR	AA	25	0	1	10	18	0	23	18	2	2.0	9.0	23	45%	.254
2017	SYR	AAA	25	3	1	10	36	0	42[1]	33	1	3.0	8.9	42	46%	.281
2018	SYR	AAA	26	1	2	1	14	0	17	16	1	2.1	8.5	16	46%	.306
2018	WAS	MLB	26	4	1	0	40	0	47[2]	43	4	2.8	8.9	47	36%	.300
2019	WAS	MLB	27	6	9	1	78	0	71[1]	64	5	3.3	10.2	81	41%	.326
2020	WAS	MLB	28	3	2	4	49	0	52	47	7	3.1	9.8	57	40%	.296

Comparables: Lou Trivino, Dustin Antolin, Jeremy Horst

There are worse things for a bullpen arm with a wicked changeup who doesn't throw four-seamers than having Fernando Rodney sitting next to you for much of the year. Suero managed to put together a respectable, if unspectacular season, though that descriptor made him one of the better arms in the Nationals bullpen in the first half. Each success should be caveated with an asterisk: He had a career-high strikeout rate (though also had an increase in walk rate) and increased his ground-ball percentage (though also had a subsequent rise in BABIP), while retaining a non-elite but non-disastrous WHIP. Mostly, like his mentor, he should be kept away from left-handed hitters and out of high-leverage spots.

YEAR	TEAM	LVL	AGE	WHIP	ERA	DRA	WARP	MPH	FB%	WHF	CSP
2017	HAR	AA	25	1.00	1.96	2.91	0.5				
2017	SYR	AAA	25	1.11	1.70	3.18	1.0				
2018	SYR	AAA	26	1.18	3.71	4.01	0.2				
2018	WAS	MLB	26	1.22	3.59	4.29	0.3	94.2	79.9	11.9	51.1
2019	WAS	MLB	27	1.26	4.54	3.64	1.3	95.4	72.2	14.7	50.5
2020	WAS	MLB	28	1.24	3.68	3.70	1.0	94.4	75.3	13.8	51.1

Wander Suero, continued

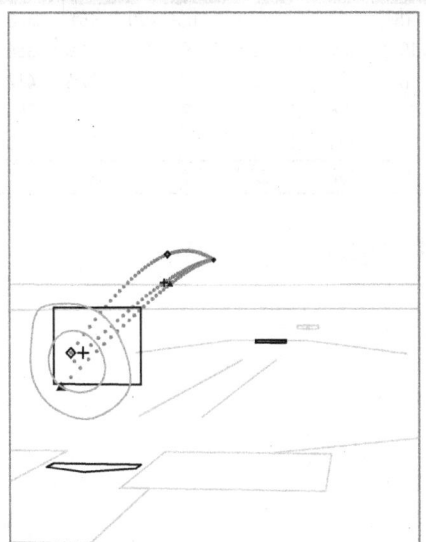
Pitch Shape vs LHH

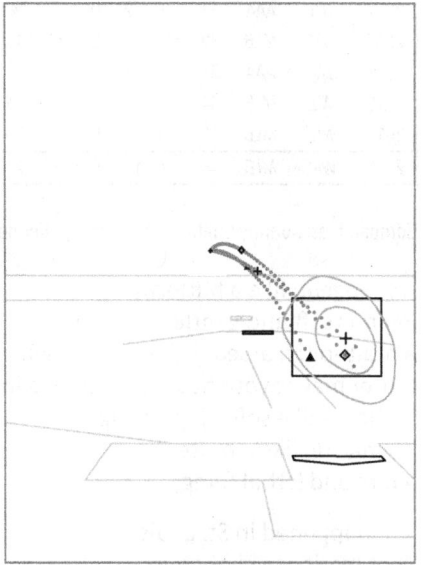
Pitch Shape vs RHH

Type	Frequency	Velocity	H Movement	V Movement
● Fastball				
☐ Sinker				
+ Cutter	72.1%	93.2 [128]	3.2 [108]	-17.6 [124]
▲ Changeup	20.7%	87.8 [109]	-9 [110]	-26.2 [104]
✕ Splitter				
▽ Slider				
◇ Curveball	7.0%	79.8 [104]	11.2 [115]	-49.6 [96]
✦ Slow Curveball				
✳ Knuckleball				
▼ Screwball				

Aníbal Sánchez RHP
Born: 02/27/84   Age: 36   Bats: R   Throws: R
Height: 6'0"   Weight: 205   Origin: International Free Agent, 2001

YEAR	TEAM	LVL	AGE	W	L	SV	G	GS	IP	H	HR	BB/9	K/9	K	GB%	BABIP
2017	TOL	AAA	33	0	2	0	4	4	15^2	17	3	2.9	11.5	20	46%	.350
2017	DET	MLB	33	3	7	0	28	17	105^1	139	26	2.5	8.9	104	36%	.354
2018	GWN	AAA	34	0	1	0	2	2	6^2	9	2	5.4	12.1	9	37%	.412
2018	ATL	MLB	34	7	6	0	25	24	136^2	106	15	2.8	8.9	135	47%	.255
2019	WAS	MLB	35	11	8	0	30	30	166	153	22	3.1	7.3	134	39%	.265
2020	WAS	MLB	36	8	9	0	26	26	137	137	27	2.9	7.4	113	40%	.277

Comparables: Johnny Cueto, Matt Garza, Ian Kennedy

A changeup like a butterfly
Eephus soft and gentle as a sigh
A multi-pitch arsenal like on satin wings
Cutter makes your heart feel strange inside
It flutters like soft wings in flight
Change up like a butterfly
A rare and lethal thing

    It happened in St. Louis
That mariposa changeup
That slow and floating pitch that ties hitters up inside
Its touch is soft and gentle
Its velo cool and tender
Whenever he throws it, we think of butterflies

YEAR	TEAM	LVL	AGE	WHIP	ERA	DRA	WARP	MPH	FB%	WHF	CSP
2017	TOL	AAA	33	1.40	4.60	4.68	0.2				
2017	DET	MLB	33	1.59	6.41	6.22	-0.8	93.2	49.6	10.9	49
2018	GWN	AAA	34	1.95	10.80	7.00	-0.1				
2018	ATL	MLB	34	1.08	2.83	2.75	4.0	92.7	37.6	11.5	46.2
2019	WAS	MLB	35	1.27	3.85	4.39	2.5	92.4	35.1	10.9	46
2020	WAS	MLB	36	1.32	4.54	4.52	2.0	91.3	38	10.8	45.9

Aníbal Sánchez, continued

Pitch Shape vs LHH

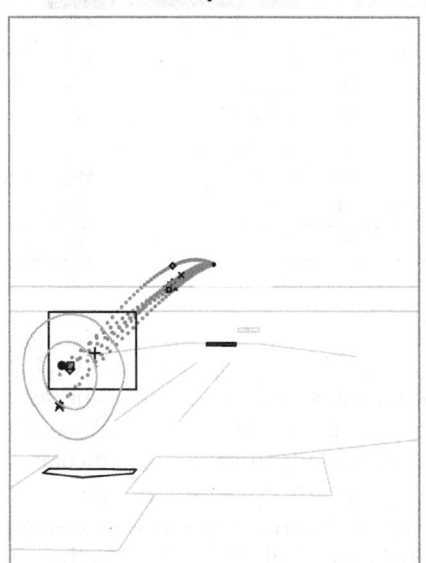

Pitch Shape vs RHH

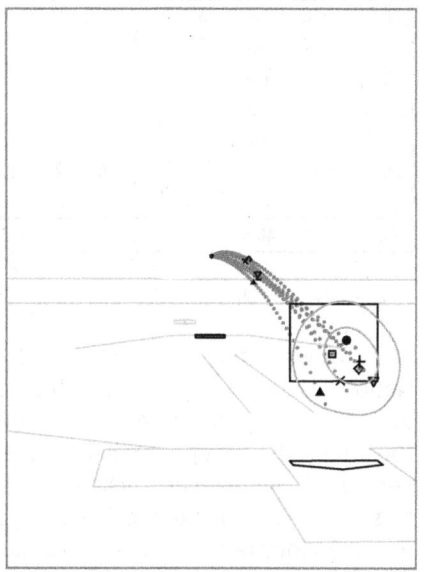

Type	Frequency	Velocity	H Movement	V Movement
● Fastball	25.5%	90.8 [95]	-3.2 [116]	-14.1 [105]
□ Sinker	9.6%	90.7 [90]	-10.3 [115]	-16.6 [113]
+ Cutter	27.8%	88.2 [97]	2.9 [106]	-20 [115]
▲ Changeup	23.5%	84.6 [98]	-12.1 [95]	-27.1 [101]
✕ Splitter	4.5%	71.1 [39]	-7.3 [102]	-39.9 [64]
▽ Slider	3.3%	83.5 [96]	5.2 [101]	-30.6 [107]
◇ Curveball	5.8%	77.1 [95]	3.6 [84]	-42.9 [110]
⊕ Slow Curveball				
✱ Knuckleball				
▼ Screwball				

Austin Voth RHP

Born: 06/26/92 Age: 28 Bats: R Throws: R
Height: 6'2" Weight: 201 Origin: Round 5, 2013 Draft (#166 overall)

YEAR	TEAM	LVL	AGE	W	L	SV	G	GS	IP	H	HR	BB/9	K/9	K	GB%	BABIP
2017	HAR	AA	25	3	4	0	10	10	54^1	63	8	2.2	7.3	44	44%	.320
2017	SYR	AAA	25	1	7	0	13	13	66^1	85	12	4.6	5.7	42	45%	.329
2018	SYR	AAA	26	6	8	0	24	24	125^2	119	13	2.9	8.4	117	42%	.295
2018	WAS	MLB	26	1	1	0	4	2	12^1	12	3	4.4	8.0	11	45%	.257
2019	HAR	AA	27	1	1	0	3	3	11^1	11	1	1.6	8.7	11	37%	.345
2019	FRE	AAA	27	3	5	0	12	12	61^1	68	7	2.2	10.0	68	41%	.345
2019	WAS	MLB	27	2	1	0	9	8	43^2	33	5	2.7	9.1	44	38%	.257
2020	WAS	MLB	28	5	5	0	41	11	89	86	17	3.0	9.3	92	39%	.291

Comparables: Alec Mills, Kyle McGowin, William Cuevas

At a time when the game is moving away from having even a fourth starter, the Nationals improbably had three fifth starters—Ross, Fedde and Voth—the last of whom did not make the World Series roster despite having the best season of the three, albeit over a smaller number of games. His curveball, in particular, generated a whiff on nearly half of all swings, and he looked sharp in three losses to Atlanta, including a one-run gem that devolved into chaos following an errant Rodney fastball finding and injuring Charlie Culberson. Like his other fifth-starter counterparts, Voth may make an attractive trade piece as the Nationals attempt to restock their infield.

YEAR	TEAM	LVL	AGE	WHIP	ERA	DRA	WARP	MPH	FB%	WHF	CSP
2017	HAR	AA	25	1.40	5.13	5.01	0.1				
2017	SYR	AAA	25	1.79	6.38	7.08	-1.0				
2018	SYR	AAA	26	1.27	4.37	3.92	2.3				
2018	WAS	MLB	26	1.46	6.57	5.14	0.0	93.1	62	9.3	51.7
2019	HAR	AA	27	1.15	4.76	5.54	-0.1				
2019	FRE	AAA	27	1.35	4.40	3.67	1.8				
2019	WAS	MLB	27	1.05	3.30	4.08	0.8	94.7	60.5	13.7	49.5
2020	WAS	MLB	28	1.30	4.39	4.39	1.3	93.8	61.2	12.9	50.8

Austin Voth, continued

Pitch Shape vs LHH
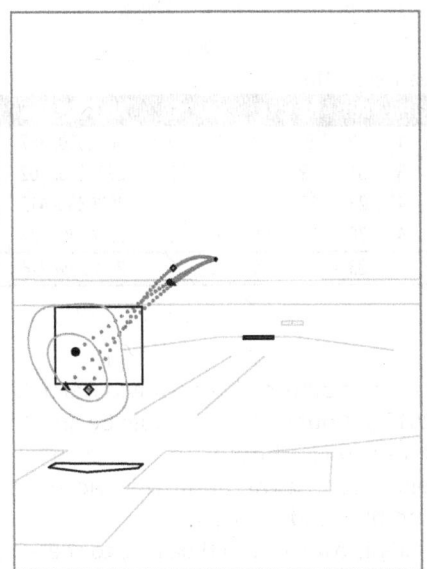

Pitch Shape vs RHH
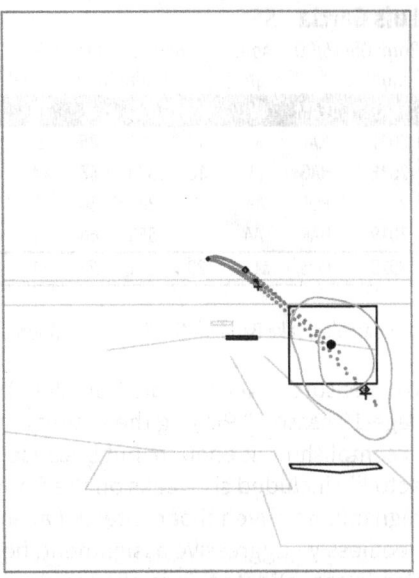

Type	Frequency	Velocity	H Movement	V Movement
● Fastball	60.5%	92.9 [102]	-3.4 [115]	-13.6 [106]
☐ Sinker				
+ Cutter	11.4%	86.8 [88]	3.2 [108]	-25.4 [95]
▲ Changeup	7.7%	86.3 [104]	-7 [120]	-23.5 [111]
✕ Splitter				
▽ Slider				
◇ Curveball	20.3%	79.6 [103]	12.3 [120]	-42.6 [110]
✦ Slow Curveball				
✱ Knuckleball				
▼ Screwball				

PLAYER COMMENTS WITHOUT GRAPHS

Luis Garcia SS
Born: 05/16/00   Age: 20   Bats: L   Throws: R
Height: 6'2"   Weight: 190   Origin: International Free Agent, 2016

YEAR	TEAM	LVL	AGE	PA	R	2B	3B	HR	RBI	BB	K	SB	CS	AVG/OBP/SLG
2017	NAT	RK	17	211	25	8	3	1	22	9	32	11	2	.302/.330/.387
2018	HAG	A	18	323	48	14	4	3	31	19	49	8	5	.297/.335/.402
2018	POT	A+	18	221	34	7	2	4	23	12	33	4	1	.299/.338/.412
2019	HAR	AA	19	553	66	22	4	4	30	17	86	11	5	.257/.280/.337
2020	WAS	MLB	20	251	21	11	1	4	23	11	50	2	1	.243/.279/.346

Comparables: Jake Bauers, Mike Trout, Elvis Andrus

We measure baseball years from July 1st to June 30th, so last year was Garcia's "age-19 season." Playing the entirety of 2019 in Double-A at 19 would be an accomplishment enough, but because of his mid-May birthday, that season actually included six weeks on the front end where he was an 18-year-old in the high minors. Given that context of an incredibly—and perhaps needlessly—aggressive assignment, he held his own. It would be nice to see Garcia consolidate things offensively, and he might not have otherworldly upside. But you can do worse betting against teenagers with quick bats who are advanced enough to survive several levels higher than they should be.

YEAR	TEAM	LVL	AGE	PA	DRC+	VORP	BABIP	BRR	FRAA	WARP
2017	NAT	RK	17	211	97	7.5	.353	1.7	2B(25): -3.0, SS(17): 0.7	0.6
2018	HAG	A	18	323	110	16.4	.343	0.7	3B(36): -4.6, SS(27): 0.4	1.0
2018	POT	A+	18	221	118	9.8	.337	-0.3	SS(40): -2.7	0.9
2019	HAR	AA	19	553	69	6.7	.299	3.1	SS(92): -3.9, 2B(38): 0.4	0.5
2020	WAS	MLB	20	251	65	-3.6	.294	-0.1	SS 0, 2B 0	-0.4

Carter Kieboom SS

Born: 09/03/97 Age: 22 Bats: R Throws: R
Height: 6'2" Weight: 190 Origin: Round 1, 2016 Draft (#28 overall)

YEAR	TEAM	LVL	AGE	PA	R	2B	3B	HR	RBI	BB	K	SB	CS	AVG/OBP/SLG
2017	AUB	A-	19	29	4	1	0	1	4	1	2	1	0	.250/.276/.393
2017	HAG	A	19	210	36	12	0	8	26	28	40	2	2	.296/.400/.497
2018	POT	A+	20	285	48	15	0	11	46	36	50	6	1	.298/.386/.494
2018	HAR	AA	20	273	36	16	1	5	23	22	59	3	1	.262/.326/.395
2019	FRE	AAA	21	494	79	24	3	16	79	68	100	5	2	.303/.409/.493
2019	WAS	MLB	21	43	4	0	0	2	2	4	16	0	0	.128/.209/.282
2020	WAS	MLB	22	420	46	19	1	14	50	38	114	1	1	.239/.316/.407

Comparables: Corey Seager, Dilson Herrera, Victor Robles

The Nationals got pure magic early on in the 2018 season by utilizing the YOLO theory of player development and bringing stud prospect Juan Soto up to the majors before schedule. They went back to the well in 2019 by calling up Kieboom, one of baseball's top prospects, in late April. He lasted only ten completely overmatched games before being sent down. It was nevertheless a successful season for him on the whole; he put up a very fine campaign as a 21-year-old in his first run at Triple-A, and is still one of the top prospects in the game. But the Nats never gave him another run in The Show, even bypassing him for a seemingly deserved September call-up. He'll get another chance in 2020, one that he's actually ready for. Major League Baseball remains very, very hard, though.

YEAR	TEAM	LVL	AGE	PA	DRC+	VORP	BABIP	BRR	FRAA	WARP
2017	AUB	A-	19	29	101	0.2	.240	0.2	SS(6): 1.1	0.2
2017	HAG	A	19	210	163	20.0	.344	-0.7	SS(45): 1.4	2.3
2018	POT	A+	20	285	159	31.4	.332	0.5	SS(56): -0.4	2.9
2018	HAR	AA	20	273	108	13.3	.324	0.5	SS(62): 2.6	1.8
2019	FRE	AAA	21	494	126	43.7	.362	1.4	SS(62): -3.7, 2B(40): 3.2	3.5
2019	WAS	MLB	21	43	62	0.0	.143	0.1	SS(10): -1.0	-0.1
2020	WAS	MLB	22	420	89	3.4	.305	-0.6	3B -3	0.0

Jake Noll 3B

Born: 03/08/94   Age: 26   Bats: R   Throws: R
Height: 6'2"   Weight: 195   Origin: Round 7, 2016 Draft (#214 overall)

YEAR	TEAM	LVL	AGE	PA	R	2B	3B	HR	RBI	BB	K	SB	CS	AVG/OBP/SLG
2017	HAG	A	23	438	51	19	2	16	67	20	64	12	4	.270/.312/.448
2017	POT	A+	23	65	5	2	1	1	7	5	12	0	1	.190/.250/.310
2018	POT	A+	24	289	47	12	3	8	46	19	51	3	1	.302/.353/.460
2018	HAR	AA	24	260	35	8	1	3	26	14	39	4	1	.278/.328/.359
2019	FRE	AAA	25	489	69	24	0	11	54	26	89	5	2	.285/.327/.410
2019	WAS	MLB	25	13	1	1	0	0	2	1	4	0	0	.167/.231/.250
2020	WAS	MLB	26	189	18	7	0	5	20	9	43	1	0	.237/.282/.365

Comparables: Dale Long, Harry Agganis, Kelby Tomlinson

A little known addendum to the Saving America's Pastime Act legalized human cloning in exigent circumstances, such as when an MLB team has an MVP-caliber third baseman in a walk year. Enter Noll. Built using Ryan Zimmerman's DNA in a process known as somatic cell roster expansion and transplantation, Noll didn't match his progenitor's impressive 2005 minor league stint, instead posting respectable, but not explosive, numbers in Fresno. Still, he earned a cup of coffee look with the Nationals out of spring training, strolling into his first RBI as an off-brand Zimm—not as Mr. Walkoff but as Mr. Walkoff Walk.

YEAR	TEAM	LVL	AGE	PA	DRC+	VORP	BABIP	BRR	FRAA	WARP
2017	HAG	A	23	438	124	18.0	.280	-1.5	2B(88): 0.8	2.1
2017	POT	A+	23	65	52	-2.1	.217	-0.6	2B(16): -0.5	-0.2
2018	POT	A+	24	289	135	20.1	.346	1.7	3B(42): 0.4, 1B(16): 0.4	2.0
2018	HAR	AA	24	260	101	7.7	.318	1.8	3B(63): 8.5, 2B(1): 0.0	2.0
2019	FRE	AAA	25	489	86	7.4	.331	4.6	3B(51): -1.3, 1B(50): -4.4	0.3
2019	WAS	MLB	25	13	69	-0.2	.250	0.2	1B(2): 0.0, 3B(1): -0.1	0.0
2020	WAS	MLB	26	189	68	-3.9	.285	-0.1	1B -2, 3B 0	-0.6

Raudy Read C

Born: 10/29/93 Age: 26 Bats: R Throws: R
Height: 6'0" Weight: 170 Origin: International Free Agent, 2011

YEAR	TEAM	LVL	AGE	PA	R	2B	3B	HR	RBI	BB	K	SB	CS	AVG/OBP/SLG
2017	HAR	AA	23	442	44	25	1	17	61	27	79	2	0	.265/.312/.455
2017	WAS	MLB	23	11	1	0	0	0	0	0	3	0	0	.273/.273/.273
2018	HAR	AA	24	161	14	9	2	3	24	11	30	0	0	.286/.335/.435
2018	SYR	AAA	24	52	2	2	0	0	2	1	8	0	0	.260/.269/.300
2019	FRE	AAA	25	328	52	17	3	20	60	17	58	1	1	.275/.317/.546
2019	WAS	MLB	25	11	0	0	0	0	0	0	5	0	0	.091/.091/.091
2020	WAS	MLB	26	35	4	1	0	2	5	2	8	0	0	.225/.268/.419

Comparables: Zoilo Almonte, Jose Lobaton, Josmil Pinto

YEAR	TEAM	P. COUNT	FRM RUNS	BLK RUNS	THRW RUNS	TOT RUNS
2017	HAR	13457	-28.1	1.5	0.4	-27.2
2017	WAS	211	-0.2	-0.1	0.0	-0.4
2018	HAR	4606	-8.1	0.0	-0.2	-8.4
2018	SYR	1432	-2.8	0.0	-0.1	-3.0
2019	FRE	9611	-18.9	0.0	0.7	-18.4
2019	WAS	378	-0.3	-0.1	0.0	0.1
2020	WAS	1299	-1.2	-0.2	0.1	-1.3

Read came to hit balls and chew bubble gum, and unfortunately, he's not that great at one of those. The high point of his September call-up came when calling 5 2/3 innings of one-run ball for Austin Voth against Atlanta, a feat quickly (and rightly) forgotten after Charlie Culberson suffered a season-ending injury following a collision with a Fernando Rodney fastball. On the other side of the plate, Read—unlike other guys named Rowdy—cannot consistently deliver hits at the major-league level. A brutal framer who has already served one 80-game suspension for PED use, the 26-year-old truly is a callback to a different era.

YEAR	TEAM	LVL	AGE	PA	DRC+	VORP	BABIP	BRR	FRAA	WARP
2017	HAR	AA	23	442	109	21.5	.290	-3.1	C(104): -24.7	-0.4
2017	WAS	MLB	23	11	72	0.1	.375	-0.1	C(3): -0.4	0.0
2018	HAR	AA	24	161	117	5.7	.336	-2.5	C(35): -7.8	0.0
2018	SYR	AAA	24	52	79	0.0	.302	-0.1	C(10): -3.1	-0.2
2019	FRE	AAA	25	328	105	15.0	.278	-0.7	C(66): -19.5, 1B(10): 1.5	0.0
2019	WAS	MLB	25	11	69	0.1	.167	0.0	C(4): -0.4	0.0
2020	WAS	MLB	26	35	74	0.4	.249	-0.1	C -1	-0.1

Andrew Stevenson LF

Born: 06/01/94 Age: 26 Bats: L Throws: L
Height: 6'0" Weight: 192 Origin: Round 2, 2015 Draft (#58 overall)

YEAR	TEAM	LVL	AGE	PA	R	2B	3B	HR	RBI	BB	K	SB	CS	AVG/OBP/SLG
2017	HAR	AA	23	91	14	5	1	0	12	11	19	1	3	.350/.429/.438
2017	SYR	AAA	23	331	38	7	4	2	26	19	72	10	1	.252/.298/.320
2017	WAS	MLB	23	66	5	2	0	0	1	7	20	1	0	.158/.250/.193
2018	SYR	AAA	24	331	40	10	1	6	28	31	75	12	6	.235/.318/.338
2018	WAS	MLB	24	86	9	2	0	1	13	6	23	1	1	.253/.306/.320
2019	HAR	AA	25	88	12	4	0	1	5	3	24	3	0	.250/.284/.333
2019	FRE	AAA	25	333	50	17	8	6	44	24	76	10	4	.334/.383/.503
2019	WAS	MLB	25	37	4	1	1	0	0	6	11	0	1	.367/.486/.467
2020	WAS	MLB	26	133	13	5	1	2	13	9	38	4	2	.257/.312/.371

Comparables: Gus Bell, Mallex Smith, Jake Marisnick

Pity Old Man Andrew Stevenson. He's entering this season at the decrepit age of 26, having spent the previous relegated to Fresno, 2,800 miles and a world away from the majors. Stevenson proved a valuable call-up in September, but his perfectly normal development trajectory seems almost glacial compared with his fellow outfielders. Despite his advanced age, he'll continue to chase a dream—and hopefully fewer pitches out of the zone.

YEAR	TEAM	LVL	AGE	PA	DRC+	VORP	BABIP	BRR	FRAA	WARP
2017	HAR	AA	23	91	140	7.9	.459	-0.4	CF(16): -3.1, LF(3): -0.3	0.3
2017	SYR	AAA	23	331	68	-1.5	.323	2.2	CF(62): -0.2, LF(15): 1.9	0.3
2017	WAS	MLB	23	66	54	-4.3	.243	0.5	RF(14): 0.1, LF(9): -0.5	-0.2
2018	SYR	AAA	24	331	83	2.9	.296	-1.0	CF(49): -8.3, LF(25): 1.4	-0.4
2018	WAS	MLB	24	86	70	1.8	.333	0.4	LF(16): -1.4, CF(3): -0.3	-0.2
2019	HAR	AA	25	88	16	0.6	.339	1.1	LF(9): 2.5, CF(8): -0.9	-0.1
2019	FRE	AAA	25	333	99	18.2	.428	1.5	CF(52): -10.5, LF(12): -1.1	0.3
2019	WAS	MLB	25	37	75	0.0	.579	-0.2	LF(5): -0.7	-0.1
2020	WAS	MLB	26	133	77	-0.2	.353	0.2	RF 1, LF 0	0.1

Michael A. Taylor CF

Born: 03/26/91 Age: 29 Bats: R Throws: R
Height: 6'4" Weight: 212 Origin: Round 6, 2009 Draft (#172 overall)

YEAR	TEAM	LVL	AGE	PA	R	2B	3B	HR	RBI	BB	K	SB	CS	AVG/OBP/SLG
2017	HAR	AA	26	28	3	2	0	1	4	2	8	3	0	.154/.214/.346
2017	WAS	MLB	26	432	55	23	3	19	53	29	137	17	7	.271/.320/.486
2018	WAS	MLB	27	385	46	22	3	6	28	29	116	24	6	.227/.287/.357
2019	HAR	AA	28	247	36	16	2	9	35	25	69	10	6	.248/.324/.463
2019	WAS	MLB	28	97	10	7	0	1	3	7	34	6	0	.250/.305/.364
2020	WAS	MLB	29	189	20	9	1	7	22	15	65	7	2	.228/.291/.401

Comparables: Jackie Bradley Jr., Cameron Maybin, Dexter Fowler

Perhaps no other play exemplified the 2019 Washington Nationals more than Taylor catching the last out of NLDS Game 5 against the Dodgers—a pretty, desperate catch—followed by the centerfielder confusedly offering his teammates the ball as if to say, "What now?"

He spent much of his season as Michael AA. Taylor, buried in Harrisburg like so many former Pennsylvania governors. Gone, but not forgotten by the Nats faithful who remembered his tough performance in the 2017 NLDS, including a Game 4 grand slam into a Wrigley basket. Taylor's performance at the plate has always been his issue, striking out more than 30 percent of the time, though this year he at least hit the ball harder than his previous seasons, albeit over a small sample size. Now finally out of options, the 2009 draft pick still has two years left until free agency, and he's running out of time to show other teams he can be more than a defensive replacement who happens to heat up when the weather gets cold.

YEAR	TEAM	LVL	AGE	PA	DRC+	VORP	BABIP	BRR	FRAA	WARP
2017	HAR	AA	26	28	54	-0.9	.176	0.4	CF(5): 0.1	0.0
2017	WAS	MLB	26	432	93	26.7	.363	3.1	CF(111): 12.6, RF(2): -0.2	2.7
2018	WAS	MLB	27	385	67	1.4	.320	1.3	CF(113): 8.9, 1B(1): 0.0	0.8
2019	HAR	AA	28	247	121	15.9	.315	3.9	CF(42): -1.2, RF(6): -0.1	1.5
2019	WAS	MLB	28	97	58	-2.0	.396	-0.6	CF(25): 0.0, RF(7): -0.8	-0.3
2020	WAS	MLB	29	189	78	0.8	.323	0.4	CF 2, RF 0	0.3

Aaron Barrett RHP

Born: 01/02/88   Age: 32   Bats: R   Throws: R
Height: 6'3"   Weight: 230   Origin: Round 9, 2010 Draft (#266 overall)

YEAR	TEAM	LVL	AGE	W	L	SV	G	GS	IP	H	HR	BB/9	K/9	K	GB%	BABIP
2018	AUB	A-	30	2	0	0	20	0	20^2	13	0	3.5	11.3	26	60%	.250
2019	HAR	AA	31	0	2	31	50	0	52^1	39	6	2.8	10.7	62	52%	.256
2019	WAS	MLB	31	0	0	0	3	0	2^1	5	1	15.4	3.9	1	27%	.400
2020	WAS	MLB	32	1	1	0	25	0	26	28	6	5.0	8.1	23	43%	.293

Comparables: Nate Karns, AJ Ramos, Nick Vincent

Baseball can be an unkind sport. Barrett missed almost four seasons after undergoing Tommy John surgery and then fracturing his arm so catastrophically that the team sequestered the video of the injury. After spending the season in Double-A, he returned to the majors as a September call-up and posted a hitless inning in his debut, including a strikeout looking to Ronald Acuña Jr. He's able to induce swings and misses with his secondary pitches, though the velocity was still low on the few pitches he got to throw. Unless the winter gives him time to find his fastball, Barrett will remain a feel-good story that fans may not feel so good about when he faces major-league hitting.

YEAR	TEAM	LVL	AGE	WHIP	ERA	DRA	WARP	MPH	FB%	WHF	CSP
2018	AUB	A-	30	1.02	1.74	3.67	0.3				
2019	HAR	AA	31	1.05	2.75	3.46	0.7				
2019	WAS	MLB	31	3.86	15.43	4.17	0.0	92.4	70.6	4.4	36.7
2020	WAS	MLB	32	1.64	6.50	5.97	-0.2	91.5	70	4.4	36.4

Tim Cate LHP

Born: 09/30/97 Age: 22 Bats: L Throws: L
Height: 6'0" Weight: 185 Origin: Round 2, 2018 Draft (#65 overall)

YEAR	TEAM	LVL	AGE	W	L	SV	G	GS	IP	H	HR	BB/9	K/9	K	GB%	BABIP
2018	AUB	A-	20	2	3	0	9	8	31	34	1	2.9	7.5	26	45%	.333
2018	HAG	A	20	0	3	0	4	4	21	23	4	2.6	8.1	19	44%	.306
2019	HAG	A	21	4	5	0	13	13	70^1	61	2	1.7	9.3	73	57%	.309
2019	POT	A+	21	7	4	0	13	13	73^1	71	4	2.3	8.1	66	61%	.324
2020	WAS	MLB	22	2	2	0	33	0	35	34	5	3.8	7.0	27	50%	.277

Comparables: Ranger Suárez, Jeff Locke, Patrick Sandoval

Cate is a southpaw who spins a mean, mean curveball. That alone is enough to net him a lot of per diems because lefty relievers with a wipeout breaker are pillars of the modern baseball architecture. The former UConn ace is going to need an extra something that he doesn't have right now to be effective in a big-league rotation, though. Options include a couple extra ticks on his fastball, a big improvement to a fringy change, a new third pitch like a cutter or invention of a time machine to travel back to the dead-ball era.

YEAR	TEAM	LVL	AGE	WHIP	ERA	DRA	WARP	MPH	FB%	WHF	CSP
2018	AUB	A-	20	1.42	4.65	5.74	-0.2				
2018	HAG	A	20	1.38	5.57	5.20	0.0				
2019	HAG	A	21	1.05	2.82	3.63	1.3				
2019	POT	A+	21	1.23	3.31	5.29	-0.3				
2020	WAS	MLB	22	1.39	4.35	4.57	0.3				

Wil Crowe   RHP

Born: 09/09/94   Age: 25   Bats: R   Throws: R
Height: 6'2"   Weight: 240   Origin: Round 2, 2017 Draft (#65 overall)

YEAR	TEAM	LVL	AGE	W	L	SV	G	GS	IP	H	HR	BB/9	K/9	K	GB%	BABIP
2017	AUB	A-	22	0	0	0	7	7	20²	18	3	1.3	6.5	15	52%	.250
2018	POT	A+	23	11	0	0	16	15	87	71	6	3.1	8.1	78	47%	.267
2018	HAR	AA	23	0	5	0	5	5	26¹	31	4	5.5	5.1	15	44%	.325
2019	HAR	AA	24	7	6	0	16	16	95¹	85	8	2.1	8.4	89	50%	.294
2019	FRE	AAA	24	0	4	0	10	10	54	66	7	4.3	6.8	41	42%	.337
2020	WAS	MLB	25	2	2	0	33	0	35	36	6	3.7	6.9	27	44%	.286

Comparables: Erick Fedde, Dillon Tate, Mike Parisi

Crowe's quick path to the majors was sidetracked by an off-key decimette of starts in the Pacific Coast League. To be fair to the former Gamecock, the 2019 PCL frequently resembled what baseball would look like if played on the moon. Fresno gave up 6.57 runs per game as a team, and that was only fourth-worst in the league. In more normal conditions, he's just about ready to break into the majors, with a low-to-mid-90s fastball complemented by a slider, changeup and curveball. Altogether, it's your standard mid-rotation upside.

YEAR	TEAM	LVL	AGE	WHIP	ERA	DRA	WARP	MPH	FB%	WHF	CSP
2017	AUB	A-	22	1.02	2.61	3.71	0.4				
2018	POT	A+	23	1.16	2.69	4.17	1.2				
2018	HAR	AA	23	1.78	6.15	7.17	-0.6				
2019	HAR	AA	24	1.12	3.87	4.50	0.5				
2019	FRE	AAA	24	1.70	6.17	6.16	0.3				
2020	WAS	MLB	25	1.45	4.94	4.85	0.2				

Seth Romero   LHP
Born: 04/19/96   Age: 24   Bats: L   Throws: L
Height: 6'3"   Weight: 240   Origin: Round 1, 2017 Draft (#25 overall)

YEAR	TEAM	LVL	AGE	W	L	SV	G	GS	IP	H	HR	BB/9	K/9	K	GB%	BABIP
2017	AUB	A-	21	0	1	0	6	6	20	19	0	2.7	14.4	32	40%	.404
2018	HAG	A	22	0	1	0	7	7	25^1	20	3	2.8	12.1	34	45%	.279
2020	WAS	MLB	24	2	2	0	33	0	35	35	6	3.6	9.4	36	39%	.311

Comparables: Matt Hall, Caleb Smith, Steven Matz

A career every bit as troubled as his arm is talented. Romero was dismissed from the University of Houston baseball team three years ago for decking a teammate, after a long list of prior infractions. The Nationals still drafted him in the first round, because when you're a lefty with the potential for three plus pitches, you can get away with quite a lot. He proceeded to get sent home during spring training in 2018 for staying out too late at night, and promptly blew out his elbow when he actually got on the mound later that summer. Romero missed the entire 2019 season recovering from Tommy John surgery; a year where he wasn't in the news counts as a win here. He enters his age-24 season with a whopping 47 1/3 pro innings, all at Low-A or below, and tons of injury and makeup concerns. But somewhere down there a wealth of talent remains too.

YEAR	TEAM	LVL	AGE	WHIP	ERA	DRA	WARP	MPH	FB%	WHF	CSP
2017	AUB	A-	21	1.25	5.40	3.16	0.5				
2018	HAG	A	22	1.11	3.91	2.93	0.7				
2020	WAS	MLB	24	1.41	4.71	4.88	0.2				

Jackson Rutledge RHP

Born: 04/01/99 Age: 21 Bats: R Throws: R
Height: 6'8" Weight: 250 Origin: Round 1, 2019 Draft (#17 overall)

YEAR	TEAM	LVL	AGE	W	L	SV	G	GS	IP	H	HR	BB/9	K/9	K	GB%	BABIP
2019	AUB	A-	20	0	0	0	3	3	9	4	2	3.0	6.0	6	42%	.091
2019	HAG	A	20	2	0	0	6	6	27¹	14	0	3.6	10.2	31	46%	.222
2020	WAS	MLB	21	2	2	0	33	0	35	35	5	3.8	7.8	30	41%	.292

Comparables: Parker Markel, José Castillo, Keyvius Sampson

The Twitter account @J_Cheddar34 could only be run by a cheese-loving boomer or a pitcher who throws really hard like Rutledge does. The towering righty ended up in junior college after a hip injury sidetracked his career at Arkansas. He made the most of his newfound draft eligibility, mixing four-seamers and two-seamers ticking into the upper-90s with a new power slider that quickly projected out to plus, and adding the occasional curve and change. It's stuff that could front a rotation some day, although all the usual caveats about command and injuries apply.

YEAR	TEAM	LVL	AGE	WHIP	ERA	DRA	WARP	MPH	FB%	WHF	CSP
2019	AUB	A-	20	0.78	3.00	3.55	0.2				
2019	HAG	A	20	0.91	2.30	3.40	0.6				
2020	WAS	MLB	21	1.43	4.75	4.91	0.2				

LINEOUTS

Hitters

HITTER	POS	TEAM	LVL	AGE	PA	R	2B	3B	HR	RBI	BB	K	SB	CS	AVG/OBP/SLG	DRC+	WARP
Tres Barrera	C	HAR	AA	24	403	42	23	0	8	46	36	69	1	2	.249/.323/.381	118	2.7
	C	WAS	MLB	24	2	0	0	0	0	0	0	0	0	0	.000/.000/.000	96	0.0
Gage Canning	OF	HAG	A	22	44	7	1	0	1	5	3	13	6	0	.244/.295/.341	78	-0.2
	OF	POT	A+	22	410	44	17	6	3	40	32	114	8	4	.238/.310/.341	88	0.0
Jeremy De La Rosa	OF	NAT	Rk	17	99	14	1	2	2	10	12	29	3	2	.232/.343/.366	85	-0.1
Wilmer Difo	INF	WAS	MLB	27	144	15	2	0	2	8	12	29	0	1	.252/.315/.313	74	0.1
	INF	FRE	AAA	27	261	48	14	3	4	30	25	51	13	5	.300/.369/.438	94	1.2
Cole Freeman	CF	POT	A+	24	534	82	27	3	3	49	53	60	31	6	.311/.394/.404	150	4.5
Yadiel Hernandez	OF	FRE	AAA	31	508	87	22	1	33	90	63	106	7	5	.323/.406/.604	146	2.9
Spencer Kieboom	C	HAR	AA	28	188	12	7	0	1	14	18	35	0	0	.196/.271/.256	76	0.4
Drew Mendoza	1B	HAG	A	21	239	23	12	0	4	25	34	57	3	0	.264/.377/.383	127	0.8
Viandel Pena	2B	NAT	Rk	18	154	27	10	3	0	15	21	31	6	3	.359/.455/.481	188	1.8
Israel Pineda	C	HAG	A	19	411	48	12	0	7	35	30	102	1	2	.217/.278/.305	68	0.7
Matt Reynolds	UT	FRE	AAA	28	449	65	29	4	16	55	64	95	8	2	.295/.401/.521	119	2.3
Adrian Sanchez	INF	WAS	MLB	28	32	3	0	0	0	1	1	10	0	0	.226/.250/.226	61	0.0
	INF	HAR	AA	28	282	43	19	1	6	36	19	39	11	5	.316/.365/.469	157	3.0

Former $3.9 million bonus baby **Yasel Antuna** had a lost season on the road back from 2018 Tommy John surgery. He remains one of the system's top prospects, which is one part a nod to his upside and two parts damnation of the rest of the system. ⓧ Washington needed an emergency fourth catcher in September due to Kurt Suzuki's bad elbow and called up prospect **Tres Barrera**. He got into two games, both in the late innings of blowouts, and decades from now he will get to show his future grandchildren his World Series ring because of it. ⓧ If we had asked you before you opened this chapter whether **Gage Canning** was a white-shoe law firm that Sam Seaborn used to work at or a fourth outfielder prospect, would you have known? ⓧ He's a mile away from the majors, but the Nationals showed how much they like **Jeremy De La Rosa** by challenging him with a stateside assignment as a 17-year-old making his pro debut. He held his own. ⓧ Nothing says "juiced-ball era" like a **Wilmer Difo** second-deck home run against the Mets. In April. Somehow they kept playing baseball anyway. ⓧ No, we can't really explain what **Cole Freeman** was doing in the Carolina League long enough to contend for the batting title, either. He's speedy, puts the bat on the ball and can play both the infield and outfield, so the wheel is probably stopping on "utility player" here. ⓧ Former Cuban star **Yadiel Hernandez** had an absolute monster season in Triple A with the happy fun ball after taking a few years to adjust to the American minors. He deserves a shot at outfield time against righties on a bad team to be named later. ⍟ **Spencer Kieboom** belongs to an exclusive fraternity of marginal major-league catchers with less-marginal, middle-infielder brothers. It's actually just a table for two with Jhonatan Solano. Austin Romine used to be invited but is no longer welcome. ⍟ If you believe in nominative determinism, **Drew Mendoza** will only be a .200 hitter, which would be a real problem for his profile since he's actually a hulking college first baseman. ⍟ **Viandel Pena** is tiny—he is listed at 5-foot-8 and 148 pounds, and sometimes those listings are generous. You probably guessed that there isn't much power here, and you'd be right, but he has feel for the bat and can play the middle infield. ⍟ **Israel Pineda** is a glove-over-bat teenaged catching prospect, which means he could be anything from a minor-league coach to a major-league relief pitcher to an honorary Molina brother by the time he reaches his thirties. Oh, the possibilities of youth. ⍟ **Matt Reynolds** did everything he normally does and then some in 2019: played six positions in Triple A, set a new career high in homers and even pitched twice. But he failed to make the majors while doing so, breaking a four-year streak of being rostered that started when the Mets purchased his contract during the 2015 NLDS. ⍟ There's a cup of coffee, and then there's a caffeine overdose. **Adrían Sanchez** spent much of 2019 traversing the highway between DC and Harrisburg, serving as a replacement-level infielder when the Nats put up a crooked number or had one put up against them.

Pitchers

PITCHER	TEAM	LVL	AGE	W	L	SV	G	GS	IP	H	HR	BB/9	K/9	K	GB%	WHIP	ERA	DRA	WARP
Joan Adon	HAG	A	20	11	3	0	22	21	105	93	8	3.8	7.7	90	46%	1.30	3.86	5.27	-0.1
Michael Blazek	FRE	AAA	30	2	2	1	34	1	38^2	44	9	3.7	9.8	42	29%	1.55	6.05	5.40	0.3
	WAS	MLB	30	0	0	0	4	0	5	6	1	9.0	0.0	0	14%	2.20	7.20	9.31	-0.2
James Bourque	HAR	AA	25	3	0	6	14	0	20^1	17	1	2.7	14.6	33	37%	1.13	1.33	3.45	0.3
	FRE	AAA	25	4	1	3	33	0	43^2	41	6	6.2	10.9	53	47%	1.63	5.56	3.93	1.0
	WAS	MLB	25	0	0	0	1	0	0^2	3	0	27.0	0.0	0	75%	7.50	54.00	4.69	0.0
Ben Braymer	HAR	AA	25	4	4	0	13	13	79	56	7	2.4	7.9	69	34%	0.97	2.51	3.29	1.6
	FRE	AAA	25	0	6	0	13	13	60	81	18	5.2	7.1	47	33%	1.93	7.20	9.19	-1.4
Matt Cronin	HAG	A	21	0	0	1	17	0	22	11	1	4.5	16.8	41	20%	1.00	0.82	2.34	0.6
Mason Denaburg	NAT	Rk	19	1	1	0	7	4	20^1	23	1	6.2	8.4	19	48%	1.82	7.52	8.54	-0.6
Tyler Dyson	AUB	A-	21	2	1	0	8	8	31^2	20	1	2.3	4.0	14	50%	0.88	1.14	4.11	0.4
Steven Fuentes	POT	A+	22	1	1	0	8	0	17	8	0	3.7	13.8	26	46%	0.88	0.53	2.36	0.5
	HAR	AA	22	5	4	0	15	11	63^2	63	1	2.1	8.9	63	58%	1.23	2.69	4.61	0.2
David Hernandez	SWB	AAA	34	0	1	0	8	0	7	5	1	10.3	14.1	11	40%	1.86	7.71	4.70	0.1
	CIN	MLB	34	2	5	2	47	0	42^2	53	7	4.2	11.2	53	32%	1.71	8.02	6.09	-0.3
Tony Sipp	WAS	MLB	35	1	2	0	36	0	21	19	1	3.9	7.7	18	38%	1.33	4.71	5.37	0.0
Jonny Venters	HAR	AA	34	0	0	0	10	0	7	6	0	7.7	5.1	4	74%	1.71	1.29	6.46	-0.2
	GWN	AAA	34	0	0	0	7	0	7	3	0	2.6	7.7	6	81%	0.71	0.00	2.58	0.2
	ATL	MLB	34	0	0	1	9	0	4^2	9	3	15.4	13.5	7	50%	3.64	17.36	5.41	0.0
	WAS	MLB	34	0	1	0	3	0	3^1	3	0	5.4	13.5	5	89%	1.50	5.40	5.37	0.0
Austen Williams	WAS	MLB	26	0	0	0	2	0	0^1	5	2	27.0	27.0	1	40%	18.00	162.00	4.64	0.0
Eddy Yean	NAT	Rk	18	1	2	0	8	8	35^1	30	3	3.1	9.2	36	52%	1.19	3.82	3.48	1.0
	AUB	A-	18	1	1	0	2	2	11	7	0	4.1	5.7	7	44%	1.09	2.45	4.35	0.1

Joan Adon has always seemed destined to a future as a 95-and-a-slider reliever, but he stretched out into the rotation in Low-A during 2019 and held up just fine. ⓧ **Michael Blazek** was in spring training for the American Association's Lincoln Saltdogs when the Nationals purchased his contract. He would briefly and unsuccessfully pop up in the majors two months later. ⓧ **James Bourque** is memorable for his mustache and for posting worse numbers than Trevor Rosenthal, all within a span of a few depressing minutes. He, like Rosenthal, is likely to be shaved from a major-league roster soon. ⓧ **Ben Braymer** is just left-handed enough that the Nats opted to add him to their 40-man despite his poor showing in Fresno. That protected him from being eligible for the Rule 5 draft in which he would've had very little business being selected. ⓧ University of Arkansas closer **Matt Cronin** made a seamless transition to A-ball dominance after the Nationals popped him in the fourth round. He'll likely be one of the first players from the 2019 draft class to make the majors and projects as a future setup man or LOOGY, provided they still exist. ⓑ 2018 first-rounder **Mason Denaburg** has yet to make it out of the complex, and his season ended on August 3rd with shoulder problems. It's not what you want, especially when he originally fell in the draft due to injury concerns. ⓑ Fifth-round pick **Tyler Dyson** has extremely impressive raw stuff for a mid-round college pick. You can probably guess that he never really put it together in college because if you have big stuff and were actually good somewhere like the University of Florida you go a heck of a lot earlier in the draft than Dyson did. ⓑ Sleeper groundball specialist **Steven Fuentes** became a more interesting prospect when he continued to have success after a midseason conversion into the rotation. Unfortunately, the experiment came to an early end when he was hit with a suspension for stimulant usage in August. ⓑ Legend holds that if you stand in front of a bathroom mirror and recite, "It's only a forearm strain, how bad could it be?" three times, **Koda Glover** appears. Which he hasn't. All season. ⓑ **David Hernandez** has long seen his ERA balloon and contract based on how many homers he allows, and it shouldn't surprise that the rocket ball did him few favors. He can still rack up strikeouts, but between walks and hits allowed, he was quite the WHIPping boy last year. ⓑ **Andry Lara** was the highest-profile 2019 Nats international signing, and therefore is by default one of the top prospects in a system as thin as the branches of a cherry blossom tree. ⓑ If the Nationals wanted an older middle-inning reliever with inconsistent stuff, an above-4 ERA and a mediocre WHIP in **Tony Sipp**, well, Fernando Rodney was also right there. ⓑ Three games, three innings, three hits, three runs, and three-plus months on the IL (following three Tommy John surgeries): **Jonny Venters** stars in "Unearned Run: The 2019 Nationals Bullpen Story." ⓑ It is a truth universally acknowledged that a relief pitcher, in possession of a moderate slider, must be in want of the strike zone. Unfortunately for **Austen Williams**, like Lydia Bennet, he fell victim to many a rake last season before being rescued back into respectability with a long stint on the IL. ⓑ Projectable Dominican righty **Eddy Yean** was impressive in his stateside debut. He's a long way away, but intriguing.

Nationals Prospects

The State of the System
The Nats won't be flying any "Number One Org Ranking" flags anytime soon. The other flag is better anyway, and it flies forever.

The Top Ten

─────── ★ ★ ★ *2020 Top 101 Prospect* **#11** ★ ★ ★ ───────

1
Carter Kieboom   SS   OFP: 70   ETA: 2019
Born: 09/03/97   Age: 22   Bats: R   Throws: R   Height: 6'2"   Weight: 190
Origin: Round 1, 2016 Draft (#28 overall)

The Report: In most ways, Carter Kieboom had a very successful 2019. He hit over .300 at Triple-A as a 21-year-old. He continued to show a well-rounded offensive skill set, with the potential for plus hit and above-average power. He's becoming more selective at the plate, which we targeted as an area for him to improve. And he did, briefly, reach the majors.

The major league stint probably received more ink than the rest of it combined. Kieboom was called up in April to replace an injured Trea Turner. He promptly went into a massive offensive slump, wasn't great at shortstop, and got sent down about two weeks later. It was bad, but he continued chugging along for the rest of the Triple-A season, despite strangely being bypassed for a September call-up.

Kieboom's future defensive home is the biggest mystery at the moment. He's more likely to stay at shortstop than he was in the low-minors in a vacuum, but capable if unspectacular defense isn't going to unseat Trea Turner. The Nationals exposed him to a good deal of second base and a little bit of third base last season, and he projects as more than capable at both. Where he lands will be as much determined by team needs that are themselves not yet clear, and he'll likely be in the mix for a job out of spring training.

Variance: Low. We're reasonably sure he's going to be a long-term regular, even if he doesn't hit his star upside.

Mark Barry's Fantasy Take: In all likelihood, had Kieboom spent the entirety of his 2019 campaign in the minors, he'd probably be a top-fiveish dynasty prospect, hitting .303 with an OPS approaching .900 at Triple-A Fresno. But alas, he joined the big club for 11 games early in the season and was Very Not Good.

If that dampens his dynasty value in your league, though, that's great for enterprising managers. He's not going to run, so his fantasy ceiling will be capped. He's not a star, but we're still looking at a dude who should flirt with a .300 average and decent pop up the middle, which is nice.

2. Luis Garcia SS
OFP: 60 ETA: 2021
Born: 05/16/00 Age: 20 Bats: L Throws: R Height: 6'2" Weight: 190
Origin: International Free Agent, 2016

The Report: The Nationals have a knack for finding young untapped talent and putting them in the best position to succeed. Luis Garcia is the current prospect being aggressively promoted through the system, showcasing a wise-beyond-his-years baseball IQ despite his young age and lack of professional experience. There's room for growth in his frame, and he already has the confidence of a major leaguer. Probably because he's extremely close to being one.

He's a dream with the glove; swift movements, quick hands and great range. There's a natural tendency for splashy plays and his abilities at shortstop translate just as well to second and third. Versatility is Garcia's best friend, as the Nats are fully stocked in the middle infield, and while they're sticking to developing him as a shortstop, that may not be where he lands once he makes it to the big club.

At the plate, he's aggressive and contact-heavy, often jumping on the first pitch he sees. His bat-to-ball skills are there, with great barrel control, and he hits it all over the park. The approach wasn't nearly as effective in Double-A as it was at previous levels. Patience is a virtue, and it's something Garcia will have to bring to his game if he really wants to improve his hit tool. The same aggressiveness at the plate is a weapon on the basepaths; he has above-average speed and utilizes it to swipe bags whenever he can. The one weakness in his offensive profile is he's unlikely to ever hit for much power.

Variance: Medium. There were some offensive struggles, albeit minor ones, that will likely be improved upon with more experience in higher levels.

Mark Barry's Fantasy Take: Looking at Garcia's profile and production gives me strong Jean Segura vibes. Last year in this very space, Ben labeled him as a guy that could go 20/20 while sticking at shortstop, and nothing really has changed, except that Garcia is now a guy who could go 20/20 with positional eligibility all over the infield.

3. Jackson Rutledge RHP
OFP: 60 ETA: 2022
Born: 04/01/99 Age: 21 Bats: R Throws: R Height: 6'8" Weight: 250
Origin: Round 1, 2019 Draft (#17 overall)

The Report: Rutledge is a big JuCo arm in every sense, his hulking frame oozing intimidation with a double-plus fastball cashing the checks. Sitting 94-96 and touching 98 for me, the pitch is extremely lively up in the zone where he gets plenty of swings and misses as well as weak contact. There's also some deception here, as Rutledge employs surprisingly short arm action before releasing from a lowish three-quarters slot. I saw him tear up right-handed hitters, pounding his number one inside to begin counts and finishing them off with his plus slider. Easily his best secondary at present, this pitch comes in hard mid-to-upper 80s with late, tight break. But wait, there's more! His 11-5 curve could be future plus as well with a little refinement, as he can already throw it for strikes with some snap. He throws a change as well but it lags behind the rest of the arsenal. Rutledge runs into issues with his motion from time to time, unsurprisingly given his size, and does have bouts of trouble with his control and command. He's far from devoid of athleticism though, and showed me an ability to adjust when necessary and retain strength late in an outing.

Variance: High. There is give both ways; if the command and pitch mix don't develop as desired, Rutledge could be destined for the pen. If everything comes together, with his stuff he's a No. 2 or better.

Mark Barry's Fantasy Take: Yeesh. So this list gets rough in a hurry. Rutledge is a big dude with a power arm and two great pitches. His tippy-top ceiling of an SP2 will depend on his control and the development of a third pitch. He's a top 200ish guy as it stands.

4. Wil Crowe   RHP   OFP: 50   ETA: 2020
Born: 09/09/94   Age: 25   Bats: R   Throws: R   Height: 6'2"   Weight: 240
Origin: Round 2, 2017 Draft (#65 overall)

The Report: Crowe has a big, durable, starter's frame, but a high-effort reliever's delivery. There's crossfire and head whack, deception and below-average command. The fastball can get to 95 in short bursts, but sits more low 90s with the occasional distinct two-seam a tick below that. Crowe's best secondary is a power, mid-80s slider with good tilt. He commands it better than the fastball, and you could see it playing up in a role where he can throw it two out of five times or so. Crowe rounds out the arsenal with a slurvy curveball around 80 with inconsistent 11-5 shape. He can flash a tighter one for a different look both in velocity and break. The change is firm and he struggles to turn it over or get it down. Crowe very much looks the part of a major league reliever still starting in the minors, although if he can squeeze out a bit more command and improve the changeup, he could be a backend innings eater, although that's a role that doesn't really exist anymore for modern orgs.

Variance: Medium. Crowe is still starting and has been durable despite the health concerns coming out of the draft. They haven't been great or efficient starter's innings though, and he's a better fit in the pen.

Mark Barry's Fantasy Take: If Crowe sticks in the rotation, he's not going to strike out enough guys to be relevant. If he's an "average setup" guy, then uh, he's an average setup guy, which also isn't particularly of interest.

5. Mason Denaburg   RHP   OFP: 55   ETA: 2023
Born: 08/08/99   Age: 20   Bats: R   Throws: R   Height: 6'4"   Weight: 195
Origin: Round 1, 2018 Draft (#27 overall)

The Report: Drafted just a short year ago, Denaburg has not had much game experience to justify his first round status. Towards the end of his senior prep season, he was shutdown due to arm soreness, which perhaps allowed him to fall slightly to the Nationals at the end of the round. He was treated very cautiously after the draft, failing to appear in any official games while working out at their complex in West Palm Beach. In 2019, he pitched sparsely before a shoulder injury ended his season.

For someone who hasn't seen the field much in almost two years there is still plenty to dream on. The young righty has an athletic body and delivery that allows for very good movement on his pitches. Prior to being hurt, his fastball sat in the low 90s with sink, he possessed a slurvy breaking ball with two-plane break, and feel for a developing changeup. The key for now is simply getting healthy. If that's in place, he still has plenty of time to develop the tools that made him one of the top arms drafted in 2018.

Variance: Extreme. When you don't pitch, it's tough to gauge which direction you're headed in. Health questions continue to remain a theme in his evaluation, and until we see some sustained success on the mound his projection is as much a question mark as any.

Mark Barry's Fantasy Take: After getting drafted, Denaburg paid off his parents' loans with his signing bonus. That's really cool. And for that act of magnanimousness, I will press pause on the snarkiness for one spot.

6. Tim Cate   LHP   OFP: 50   ETA: 2021
Born: 09/30/97   Age: 22   Bats: L   Throws: L   Height: 6'0"   Weight: 185
Origin: Round 2, 2018 Draft (#65 overall)

The Report: Businesslike and incisive on the mound, Cate has one clear plus pitch and does very well to get the most from the rest of his arsenal. His true 12-to-6 curve is the money pitch, coming in around 80 with late and sharp break. When I saw him he seemed to have a well-constructed plan of attack against right-handed hitters, which was to pound his 90-ish fastball in on the hands to generate weak contact or set up the curve as a chase pitch down or in the dirt. The pitch flashes glove-side cut which increases the intended effect and allows him to mix in his third pitch, a changeup with some decent fade. The delivery is low effort and he repeats it well; he hardly walks anyone and his fastball command is very good already. He'll need it, of course.

Variance: Low. He's a command lefty with a well-developed curve; there's not much more ceiling but he should be fine. Worst case, he ekes out a career as a middle reliever where the fastball should play up in shorter stints.

Mark Barry's Fantasy Take: I don't know, maybe like a worse-2019 Jose Quintana? Does that do anything for you?

7. Matt Cronin   LHP   OFP: 50   ETA: Late 2020
Born: 09/20/97   Age: 22   Bats: L   Throws: L   Height: 6'2"   Weight: 195
Origin: Round 4, 2019 Draft (#123 overall)

The Report: Yeah, we're stuffing a fourth-round college reliever here. It's that kind of system, but Cronin is also a pretty interesting prospect. The Arkansas closer made a seamless transition to pro ball, continuing to dominate hitters after being assigned straight to full-season ball. He pairs a fastball that gets into the mid 90s with a high-spin curveball that already grades out as plus. Cronin has a very high-effort delivery, but he repeats it well enough, and he's been extremely difficult for hitters to pick up in both college and his brief pro experience. With two plus pitches, he has a chance to be an impact relief arm. He could also move very fast; we think he has the potential to be an in-season 2020 add for the Nats if things work out well.

Variance: Medium. The track record of college relief arms is quite mixed, which keeps it from being low. Cronin himself has an obvious lefty specialist sort of fallback as a fastball/curve lefty, but anti-LOOGY rulemaking could nerf that a bit.

Mark Barry's Fantasy Take: A college reliever who could see his destiny as a LOOGY halted by crazy anti-LOOGY laws? Where do I sign up!?

8. Drew Mendoza   1B   OFP: 50   ETA: 2021/22
Born: 10/10/97   Age: 22   Bats: L   Throws: R   Height: 6'5"   Weight: 230
Origin: Round 3, 2019 Draft (#94 overall)

The Report: Mendoza is a typical long and strong corner college slugger. He played mostly third base at FSU, and while the Nats still rolled him out there occasionally for Hagerstown, his large frame is bound for the colder corner as a professional. He might have the bat to play there, as Mendoza generates plus raw power despite a stiff swing and merely average bat speed. His track record with wood isn't outstanding, and there's significant swing-and-miss concerns at the plate, but he generally knows what to swing at, and could profile as a three true outcomes second-division first baseman. The margins are very fine with this profile however. Normally, I'd tee up a C.J. Cron reference here, but Mark is on fantasy comments, so…

Variance: High. The usual hit tool questions for a length and strength first base slugger, and Mendoza doesn't have much of a professional track record yet.

Mark Barry's Fantasy Take: I see your C.J. Cron reference and I'm not playing.

9. Seth Romero   LHP   OFP: 55   ETA: 2021
Born: 04/19/96   Age: 24   Bats: L   Throws: L   Height: 6'3"   Weight: 240
Origin: Round 1, 2017 Draft (#25 overall)

The Report: Probably the best thing that happened with Seth Romero this year is that we just didn't hear about him. The talented but troubled lefty underwent Tommy John surgery late in the 2018 season, and missed the entirety of 2019. His rehab seems to be going well, and he should return in 2020.

Before the surgery, Romero would flash three plus pitches from the left side. He would also get in trouble constantly; he was dismissed from college and sent home from his first pro spring training, both for personal misbehavior. He hasn't been on the mound all that much in the last three seasons between injuries and suspensions, and correspondingly his command profile had yet to develop much. Suffice to say, there's very substantial relief and complete flame-out risk here.

Variance: Xtreme, for many of the same reasons Jeffrey laid out in the Jay Groome report.

Mark Barry's Fantasy Take: Romero didn't punch anyone this season and he didn't get suspended. I think that should be considered an unequivocal win.

10. Yasel Antuna   SS   OFP: 55   ETA: 2023
Born: 10/26/99   Age: 20   Bats: B   Throws: R   Height: 6'0"   Weight: 170
Origin: International Free Agent, 2016

The Report: Antuna was out until late-June following late-2018 Tommy John surgery. He played three games in the GCL and was promptly shut down again until instructs. It was a totally lost season for the infielder, albeit one he could afford better than most in his age-19 season given that he got over 350 plate appearances in Low-A at age-18. Going back to our 2018 looks, he'd shown wide-ranging potential, with athletic and smooth actions and the potential to hit for both average and power. The switch-hitter couldn't actualize much yet, though. His bat was nearly useless from the port side and not all that much better from the starboard, and he wasn't consistent defensively. We're hoping a mostly lost year doesn't knock him too far off the track, because he's projectable as all hell.

Variance: Extreme, which is lower than Xtreme. Antuna doesn't have a lot of experience and hasn't hit anywhere yet.

Mark Barry's Fantasy Take: Antuna basically redshirted 2019, so if you liked him last year, nothing about this season should change your mind. He's still a top-150 or 200 dynasty guy.

The Next Ten

11. Eddy Yean   RHP
Born: 06/25/01   Age: 19   Bats: R   Throws: R   Height: 6'1"   Weight: 180
Origin: International Free Agent, 2017

So the 11th-best prospect here is a young Latin arm whose first mention within the pages of Baseball Prospectus will be in this list. Originally signed for $100K in the '17 J2 class, Yean has bulked up very quickly, with evaluators guesstimating he is around 6-foot with 210 pounds of muscle. This is a good frame, but meh at the same time, as we usually like young guys with stuff and projection, and Yean lacks that projection. The fastball is the main attraction, a potential plus offering with above-average life from a tick above three-quarters slot. The slider is the obvious out pitch, with late action that he locates well against right-handers. He does get hit harder than you expect, with his pitches finding barrels way too much for your liking. Improved command should come with more reps though, and at 18 years old, Yean has plenty of time to get those reps. It is unlikely Yean gets sent straight to full-season ball next year, and some more polish in Extended Spring could help further refine this muscular ball of clay.

12 Sterling Sharp   RHP
Born: 05/30/95   Age: 25   Bats: R   Throws: R   Height: 6'3"   Weight: 170
Origin: Round 22, 2016 Draft (#664 overall)

One of the more entertaining prospects on social media, Sharp is a bit of a throwback as a prospect. He's a sinkerballer who has put up strong ground-ball and home run rates while being generally effective despite only throwing around 88-90. He also mixes in a slider, changeup, and two-seam fastball, and all of those come in around the fringe-average to average ratio. There's no out pitch projection amongst those at present, but sometimes that can actually work for a sinkerballer. For an extreme example, Steve Givarz comped him to Aaron Cook during the Fall League, and Cook once made an All-Star team. Sharp has already vastly exceeded expectations for a 22nd-rounder out of Division II baseball, at the very least. We expect he'll be somewhere in the utility to back-of-the-rotation arm spectrum soon, with sneaky upside if he can keep getting hitters to pound it into the ground.

13 Israel Pineda   C
Born: 04/03/00   Age: 20   Bats: R   Throws: R   Height: 5'11"   Weight: 190
Origin: International Free Agent, 2016

Pineda was higher on this list last year, and a very brief glance at his season line is illustrative as to why. A big part of his prospect profile is his bat, and while he still seems to possess his underlying talents there they did not manifest themselves in games in what turned out to be a lost season in the Sally League. He's still very young, though, not turning 20 until around Opening Day, and trying to realize a hit tool projection while dealing with the various tasks of ignorance behind the dish can't be easy. He's decent enough back there already and at the plate he shows the ability to keep the bat in the zone a while and barrel up all sorts of pitches. The power isn't there yet and it is unclear whether it will ever be, but let's have him repeat the level and see where it takes us.

Washington Nationals 2020

14   Joan Adon   RHP
Born: 08/12/98   Age: 21   Bats: R   Throws: R   Height: 6'2"   Weight: 185
Origin: International Free Agent, 2016

At some point in some barely-remembered time I decided that regardless of system depth we would go 20-deep on every team with a personal cheeseball and a low minors sleeper. It allows for a certain amount of streamlining within the list process, but realistically it underplays the Rays and the Padres where we could go 30 deep without much issue, and overplays...well, the Nats system, where Jarrett yelled at me for making him come up with more than ten names. He's not wrong, and although Adon is a perfectly cromulent 95-and-a-slider guy out of the pen...perhaps, he is currently a struggling, physically maxed A-ball starter. It's a solid frame, and he'd be a neat little low minors sleeper for every other team in the NL East—eh, well he might make the Mets list, too—but it's not a prospect you should feel the need to spend a full blurb on given the high-effort delivery and the command issues. Inevitably some of this job is make-work, and Nats fans would like to read about 22 prospects too, or maybe not now, because who cares about the 14th-best prospect in a bottom-five system when you just won the World Series. Must be nice. Adon might be a seventh inning guy, but he's a ways away. We'll move on swiftly now.

15   Nick Banks   OF
Born: 11/18/94   Age: 25   Bats: L   Throws: L   Height: 6'0"   Weight: 215
Origin: Round 4, 2016 Draft (#124 overall)

Banks keeps making these lists, and I keep writing him. I'm not altogether happy about it. There's a little more there this year than in the past; he's made positive swing changes over the last year. We've spotted more power than we used to as well, and he's flashing above-average to plus raw now. He's added a lot of loft to his swing. All of this portends a possibility of an outcome where everything comes together late and he starts hitting the ball with authority around the ballpark. At present, he's still not quite there, and he's also a year older with only incremental gains to show for it. We're talking about the mere potential for big gains from a polished college bat who just turned 25 and has barely made it out of A-ball yet. It's not a high-percentage outcome, is it?

16   Steven Fuentes   RHP
Born: 05/04/97   Age: 23   Bats: R   Throws: R   Height: 6'2"   Weight: 175
Origin: International Free Agent, 2011

Fuentes is a filled-out sinker/slider righty with a low arm slot who got a 50-game ban for using a banned stimulant towards the end of the 2019 season. That wasn't the best life choice. Neither was going 20-deep in this system, but we have covered that already. Fuentes has an uptempo delivery with a tough angle and slot for righties, which are nice things we write about a pitching prospect with clear relief markers. There isn't a clear bat-misser here, which might limit the relief upside, but he's a fairly safe relief prospect given his frame, Double-A success, and low-90s sinker.

17 Jeremy De La Rosa   OF
Born: 01/16/02   Age: 18   Bats: L   Throws: L   Height: 5'11"   Weight: 160
Origin: International Free Agent, 2018

Signed for 300k as part of the Nationals' 2018 July 2nd class, De La Rosa came stateside quickly, due to his present physicality and bat control. He's already spending most of his time in corner outfield spots, and with a likely long-term landing spot in left, the pressure on his bat is already strong. There's some present pop, although the swing can get slashy and play as hit over power. Check back in a couple years, when he will probably still be on these lists regardless.

18 Tyler Dyson   RHP
Born: 12/24/97   Age: 22   Bats: R   Throws: R   Height: 6'3"   Weight: 210
Origin: Round 5, 2019 Draft (#153 overall)

I certainly admire the Nationals for taking big swings on talent every now and again. It does contribute to the system weakness, sure, but one of the ways you're going to dig out of that hole is by hitting on the Tyler Dysons of the world. The Nats drafted Dyson in June after a college career where he was often injured or not that good (although he did super-shove as a freshman in the College World Series clincher), and signed him for $500,000, well-above slot for the fifth round. He's a three-pitch righty who gets into the mid 90s and even a little higher, which is a lot better than you're usually getting from a fifth-round SEC starting pitcher. There's substantial fastball/slider reliever vibes in the profile, and he was repeating the trick of not really striking anyone out despite the stuff in pro ball, but at least there's some real upside here.

19 Nick Raquet   LHP
Born: 12/12/95   Age: 24   Bats: R   Throws: L   Height: 6'0"   Weight: 215
Origin: Round 3, 2017 Draft (#103 overall)

A former third-rounder, Raquet had a good enough time repeating High-A this year, but he's already 23 and how he does in Double-A first time around will be instructive. The stuff isn't terrible with a fastball sitting low 90s, touching higher, and a low-80s slider that has nice tight break when it's right. He's inconsistent with the slider, though, and can be inconsistent in general. His change and curve aren't too reliable either and on my look he appeared to begin tiring at around 70 pitches. The delivery is a high-effort crossfire deal and his command can suffer because of it. He's a reliever to my eye but he could make it. Being a lefty always helps.

20

Jackson Tetreault   RHP
Born: 06/03/96   Age: 24   Bats: R   Throws: R   Height: 6'5"   Weight: 189
Origin: Round 7, 2017 Draft (#223 overall)

So we are probably about done waiting for the lean, 7th-round JuCo draftee to become a backend starting pitcher now. Tetreault is still on the skinny side, with command and change issues. The fastball still sits either side of 90, touching 94 or so, with good sink and occasional, possibly accidental, cut. There's a short, tight curve around 80, and a too-firm change. It more or less is what it is now, and what it is is the 20th best prospect in a bottom five system. There might be some middle relief utility here, and it's still a good frame, but that means more when you are 21 instead of 23. Life comes at you fast. Faster if you are a pitching prospect.

Personal Cheeseball

PC

Cole Freeman   2B/OF
Born: 09/27/94   Age: 25   Bats: R   Throws: R   Height: 5'9"   Weight: 175
Origin: Round 4, 2017 Draft (#133 overall)

In some ways, the cheeseball spot was made for players like Freeman. He was a 2017 fourth-round priority senior sign out of LSU. He's listed at 5-foot-9 and 175 pounds, likely generously. He's a slap-and-dash hitter. He's a second baseman who has picked up the outfield. He put up good offensive numbers in the Carolina League, but he was 24 in the Carolina League. He went to the Arizona Fall League, but as we've been discussing for many thousands of words already, the Nationals don't really have the type of prospect depth that you'd usually send to the AFL. As the prospect world's resident hype man on both Jeff McNeil and Nick Madrigal I certainly have an affinity for this general profile, hence the cheeseball designation. Freeman absolutely has a path to the majors as a utility type as long as he keeps hitting singles, but it's a tough route, and it's hard to realistically project him as a regular when you're already 25 and haven't seen the high minors yet. Perhaps he'll prove us wrong yet again.

Low Minors Sleeper

LMS

Viandel Pena   IF
Born: 11/22/00   Age: 19   Bats: B   Throws: R   Height: 5'8"   Weight: 148
Origin: International Free Agent, 2017

What do you do for a low-minors sleeper in a system where the guys we originally pegged for this ended up fairly high up the list? We had two options for this spot: Pena, who put up a shiny average in complex league ball, but is a tiny dude who correspondingly doesn't hit the ball very hard yet, or J2 pitcher Andry Lara, which would basically be a blind shot based on his signing bonus. We went with Pena. Honestly, our feedback on Pena was that he's probably a utility guy prospect, but that's better than Lara, for whom we have more or less nothing. Be forewarned that Pena could get the bat blown out of his hands in the Penn League or the Sally this year given his frame and swing, and his spot here is a complete indictment of the system.

Top Talents 25 and Under (as of 4/1/2020)

1. Juan Soto
2. Victor Robles
3. Carter Kieboom
4. Luis Garcia
5. Jackson Rutledge
6. Wil Crowe
7. Mason Denaburg
8. Tim Cate
9. Matt Cronin
10. Drew Mendoza

The Nationals packed a lot of narrative into their historic 2019 season, but perhaps the thing that they'll be most remembered for is being *old*. Old as the hills. Old as the Pixies "Doolittle" album. Organizationally, being this old is a problem, an indication of the farm system's weakness, particularly when injuries early in the season highlighted their vulnerability in replacing key players. It's also a problem–one that speaks to our relationship to professional athletes, and the commodification of their bodies–that it's considered normal to act like anyone over 30 is a breath away from crumbling into dust. Noted *viejo* Max Scherzer has explicitly tied that tendency to teams devaluing older players–and not wanting to pay free agents their worth.

The Nationals won the World Series with a roster whose average age was 30, with Howie Kendrick and Aníbal Sánchez and Fernando Rodney, and with two young players likely familiar to everyone reading this. So, without further ado, meet two guys you probably already know:

If you're going to have a team that's older than the Appalachians and only have two young players, be glad one is Juan Soto. Soto is everything his 2018 ROY-caliber season promised he'd be. Last season, his two main weaknesses were hitting breaking pitches and his defense in left field, a position he learned while in the majors having only played a handful of games in the minors there. This season, he responded by continuing to hit fastballs with a vigor that will surely haunt Josh Hader (and Gerrit Cole, and Justin Verlander, and and and…), and improved his ability to hit everything but sliders, including going from struggling against changeups to demolishing them. (It should perhaps soothe Kershaw to know Soto hits sliders off southpaws somewhat better than righties.) Defensively, he benefited from the mentoring of the many older players on the Nats, most notably Gerardo Parra, going from a defensive liability to an asset, all while keeping his elite offensive numbers.

    Victor Robles would be the young outfielder on the Nats everyone was talking about…if not for Juan Soto. Robles struggled a bit more at the plate this year than he did during his September call-up last season, hitting respectably, stealing the number of bases one would expect from a guy with 95th-percentile speed, and getting hit with an Utley-ian, Espinosa-esque number of pitches. His defensive numbers are consistently elite, including a league-leading number of outfield assists and putouts.

Part 3: Featured Articles

The Baseball Is Juiced (Again)

Robert Arthur

This article originally appeared at Baseball Prospectus on April 5, 2019.

It started when the normally reliable Chris Sale got lit up for three homers by the Mariners in the Red Sox's season opener. It was part of a record number of taters that flew on Opening Day, as starters from Sale to Zack Greinke were taken deep by the handful. Then Christian Yelich hit a home run in each of his first four games, tying yet another MLB record, this one for consecutive games with a dinger to start a season.

It didn't take long for fans and players to begin whispering and tweeting about the baseballs being juiced again. It's early yet for us to come to any definitive conclusion about the 2019 season, but preliminary data shows that the baseball has returned to its aerodynamic peak. Whether that means this season will smash home run records like 2017 did remains to be seen.

Before home run explosion over the last few years, no one worried too much about the baseball's air resistance. While MLB and Rawlings (the company that manufactures the official baseballs) kept track of dozens of metrics to make sure that the ball was consistent from month to month, they didn't measure drag.

But drag is incredibly important in determining how likely a hitter is to knock one out of the park. As baseballs become more aerodynamic, they travel further given a certain initial velocity. A deep fly ball that might have been caught at the warning track can instead go into the first row of the stands. A three percent change in drag coefficient can work to add about five feet to a well-hit fly ball, which can in turn increase home runs league wide by an astounding 10-15 percent.

It's possible to measure the aerodynamics of the baseball using the pitch-tracking radars currently in place in each MLB ballpark. By calculating the loss of speed from when the pitch is released to when it crosses the plate, you can directly measure the drag coefficient on the baseball. I first wrote about the role of decreasing drag in boosting home runs in 2017, and MLB's commission of scientists and statisticians later confirmed that the more aerodynamic baseballs in use that year were largely to blame for the spike in home runs. The same commission rejected some alternate hypotheses, like rising temperatures and a league-wide boost in launch angle pushing more balls over the fence.

The current era has featured some large fluctuations in drag coefficient, leading to first an explosion in 2016 and 2017, and then a dialing back of homers last year. Curious about the record-breaking home run tallies in the last few days, I used the same methodology to measure the aerodynamics of the baseballs so far in 2019.

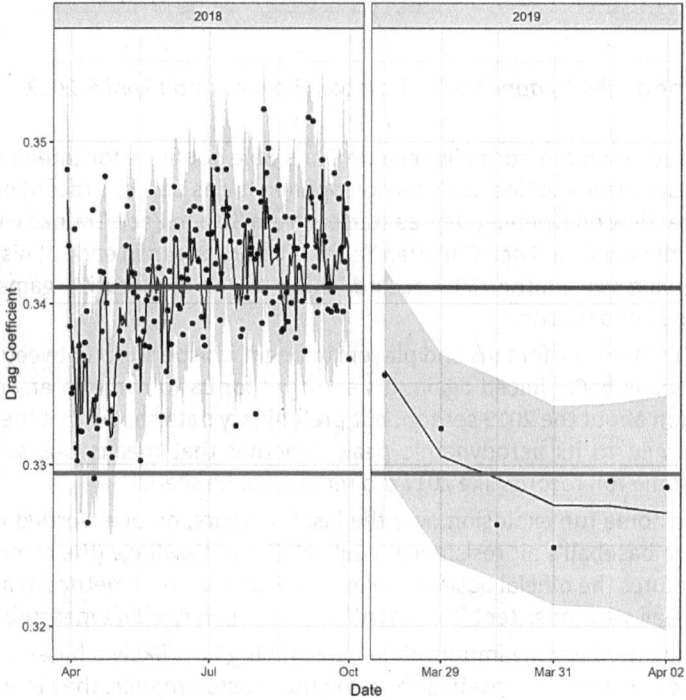

We're only a week into the 2019 season, but the drag numbers so far are among the lowest recorded in the last calendar year. With apologies for gory math, the current 2019 season average drag coefficient (the red line) would be below the 95 percent credible interval (the shaded area) for about nine-tenths of the 2018 season. (I used a Bayesian Random Walk model implemented in INLA to calculate these credible intervals, averaging the drag numbers in each game and adjusting for park.)

There were only a handful of six-day stretches in 2018 that had drag numbers below what we're seeing now, and most were in late June and early July. All of this means that 2019's data so far is quite a bit different than what we saw through most of last year.

These drag coefficients factor out the effects of temperature and air density, so they aren't a product of April cold. However, the numbers could be deceptive if the radars used to track pitches have changed from year to year. I consulted with some experts within baseball who were not aware of any specific modifications to the radar this year that could produce this pattern, but it's an important caveat of which to be aware.

On the one hand, it's only been six days, and we don't quite have the statistical basis to say that these drag coefficients are unprecedented compared to 2018. On the other hand, we've witnessed about 5,000 fastballs so far this season, so it's not as if our sample size is small. At least so far, the baseball has played like it's much more aerodynamic than it was last year. In fact, the current drag coefficient is really only comparable to 2017, when the baseballs were more aerodynamic than they had been in at least a decade.

It's not just fancy radar tracking indicating that the baseball is flying through the air more easily. The current number of home runs per game (as of this writing) is the highest it's been since the heady days of 2017, the year that teams and players broke dinger-related records everywhere you looked. That's especially remarkable considering that we're in what is typically the coldest part of the regular season, when lower temperatures and higher winds tend to suppress offense and keep balls in the air within the park. Comparing only from April to April, this year's rate of home runs per fly ball is even a little bit higher than it was in 2017.

With that said, the current measurements are no guarantee that 2019 will be another year of record-shattering homer hitting. The trouble with the drag measurements is that they are not consistent from June to August, from week to week, or even sometimes from day to day. Whether because of natural manufacturing variation or differences in the underlying supplies of cowhide and thread that go into the baseballs, drag has a tendency to fluctuate up and down over the course of a year. So the homers that fly in the first week of April wouldn't necessarily clear the fence a week later.

It's possible that this one-week drop in drag coefficient subsides and the baseball returns to its 2018 levels. On the other hand, it's almost equally probable that the ball becomes even more slippery and flies ever farther. Either way, it's clear that the baseball's air resistance is something to keep an eye on for the remainder of the 2019 season.

—*Robert Arthur is an author of Baseball Prospectus.*

The Moral Hazard of Playing It Safe

Craig Goldstein

This article originally appeared at Baseball Prospectus on August 6, 2019.

A couple days prior to the trade deadline, amidst a sea of tranquility posing as the lead up to the trade deadline, Bob Nightengale took to Twitter. Nightengale, who was probably wearing his pants backwards at the time, tweeted that MLB GMs were coming around on the idea that the unified trade deadline should be moved back from July 31 to August 15, so they could better assess their positions in the standings and whether they should buy or sell. To which I said:

This might strike some as reductive and churlish. And it might be that, but it isn't really wrong, either. Jeff Quinton wrote a great piece discussing the environmental factors that enable front offices to avoid risk without upsetting the apple cart within their own fanbases. I don't believe that it goes far enough, however. His article gives us the proper framework through which to understand why these behaviors have been allowed to seep into front offices throughout the league. Understanding the reasons behind these actions are different from excusing them, though, and GMs should not be let off the hook for their non-competitive approach to the trade deadline (much less the offseason).

⚾   ⚾   ⚾

It's fair to say that fans as a group have rarely, if ever, been pro-player. It is also fair to say that in the time during and following the Moneyball revolution, the pendulum swung from fans who cared intensely about winning in the moment (and thus might be intolerant of a rebuilding approach) to fans who supported building a team that could compete throughout multiple seasons, viewing the playoffs as a crapshoot, with the thought that getting multiple bites at the apple was a better approach than taking a bigger bite in any one season.

There's nothing wrong with that approach, and I still find merit in that argument. However, it seems that the pendulum has swung too far in that direction. Teams are overvaluing some of the individual factors that make themselves long-term contenders rather than attempting to seize a championship when given the opportunity. It's a difficult needle to thread.

And surely, they (and those in similar positions) would have liked another two weeks to clarify where they stand so as to better marshal their resources. We've all asked for a few more minutes when staring at a menu. But all of these GMs and front office personnel are where they are to make difficult decisions. They have proprietary data and internal analysts dedicated to understanding their position relative to the rest of the league, and how any move in the here and now impacts their long-term vision. To complain (if that report is accurate) that over half the season is not enough to properly assess their season is bullshit of the highest order. Move the deadline, and you'd simply have increasingly discounted trade offers because teams would be acquiring even less control of anyone they're acquiring, rental or not.

Major league front offices are behaving like the managers they lampooned two decades ago. They're effectively sacrificing a runner to second in the ninth inning—not because it's the correct move, but rather because it is safe. It used to be that the phrase "moral hazard" was used to describe general managers who made ill-fated, short-sighted decisions aimed at locking in wins and securing their jobs at the expense of their team's future. Now, general managers are guilty of committing moral hazards in the opposite direction, playing it utterly safe and terrified of becoming scapegoats.

In lieu of bold action, they opt to pussyfoot around a current window of contention, choosing instead to play the long game and stack up years of control like they're blocks in a game of Jenga. GMs pass on signing quality players in free agency because the back-end of the deal might look bad, and because they might be able to squeeze out 70 percent of the production from a player who costs a tenth as much. That's a safer investment, too, because it's also hard to prove a negative—it's impossible to prove that Manny Machado would make the Mets a playoff team in 2019-2020, but it's easy to say that the back half of Robinson Cano's contract sucks. Owners, who rule over GM's jobs, are also humans with human brain processes that will always make the so-called albatross contract uglier than the road not taken.

These days, GMs are remembered for the bad deals they make and the surplus value they generate, not the acquisition of expensive, necessary talents that meet their market worth (or fall slightly short while still providing significant on-field value). And front offices know that one or two expensive misfires can cost them their jobs, no matter how many good deals they make.

No front office exemplifies this ethos more than the Toronto Blue Jays. General Manager Ross Atkins had this to say following the Blue Jays underwhelming trade deadline:

This is by no means the first time that an executive will cite years of control to justify their actions, which is often just another way of saying "don't look at what we got, look at how much we got of it." Atkins touts quantity to elide the discussion of quality—either, that of the players acquired, or those given up. Remember: the other teams presumably value years of control, too.

Atkins also had some thoughts to offer regarding free agents back in early 2018:

This ignores, of course, whether the player can create enough value in the front end of a contract to justify the longer term of a deal, and the decline that often occurs in the back end. It also ignores whether the player can fill a need the team requires and put them in a position to compete for and win a championship. But as teams seemingly avoid contention at all, where they might end up having to consider and later justify some of these tough decisions, we still see risk-averse approaches.

Anthony Fenech's article on two trades that recently extended GM Al Avila didn't make got at this issue rather well:

> Passing on those deals was defensible: Both players had yet to break out and trading [Michael] Fulmer—a pitcher who appeared to be a future ace, no matter his injury concerns—would have taken serious gumption, opening Avila up to strong criticism.

Avoiding strong criticism is something each of us can understand as a motivation, but the avoidance of criticism only matters if that criticism is valid. In Fulmer's case, shoving his injury concerns aside affects not only the years that the team controls him (he is currently missing a full season due to Tommy John surgery) but also the quality of those seasons, as his knee and elbow injuries combined to dampen his effectiveness even when healthy enough to pitch. But it was easy to present the then-current image of Fulmer as a top of the rotation pitcher who the team had under its domain for the next five seasons as something to build around. The status quo isn't nearly as often second-guessed as a decision that disrupts it.

⚾ ⚾ ⚾

MLB GMs are risk-averse to a fault. They are ivy-educated and consulting firm-approved, and yet they can't seem to avoid leaving wins on the table in their all-consuming lust for a non-existent $/WAR championship. They are supposed to zig when everyone else zags, and not merely pay lip service to the idea of zigging through a calculated PR plan built on convincing the fan base their approach is novel when it actually apes most of their competitors. Instead they've become far more concerned with making safe, accepted-by-the-new-common-wisdom decisions, such that our prior understanding of what a moral hazard is has become inverted.

I can't blame them entirely, and not only because of the reasons that Quinton illuminated in his article, but also because of the damage wrought by the introduction of the second wild card (WC2) spot. MLB's desire to have more teams in playoff contention has sparked anti-competitive behavior. Teams know now that they do not need to swing big as they assemble their roster because there is a good chance that a mediocre team can either catch fire and capture a division, or muddle along until they back into the WC2.

Simultaneously, the one-game playoff has neutered the WC1, putting an entire season on the flip of a coin like some sort of baseball-obsessed Anton Chigurh. While the one-game playoff makes sense as a way to increase the value of winning a division, it also means that if a front office doesn't like its chances of overcoming a behemoth like the Dodgers or Astros in the offseason, they have few incentives to chase glory. Similarly, the relative inaction in the NL Central at the trade deadline—despite a wide open division—can be explained by the idea that any high-variance investment could still result in only a wild card (or worse) result, given the mere two months left in the season to make an impact.

⚾ ⚾ ⚾

As stated at the top, we should not confuse reasons for excuses. The implementation of the second wild card is just one of many environmental factors that influence how each front office operates. I am convinced that it is one of the larger factors, but I am also convinced that organizations need to shed the yoke of "efficiency at all costs" so that they can instead pursue competition, as the spirit of the game intends. Until they do, we're all deadline losers.

—*Craig Goldstein is an author of Baseball Prospectus.*

Index of Names

Abad, Fernando 49
Adon, Joan 103, 112
Antuna, Yasel 110
Banks, Nick 112
Barrera, Tres 101
Barrett, Aaron 96
Blazek, Michael 103
Bourque, James 103
Braymer, Ben 103
Cabrera, Asdrúbal 20
Canning, Gage 101
Castillo, Welington 22
Castro, Starlin 24
Cate, Tim 97, 108
Corbin, Patrick 51
Cronin, Matt 103, 109
Crowe, Wil 98, 107
De La Rosa, Jeremy 101, 113
Denaburg, Mason 103, 108
Difo, Wilmer 101
Doolittle, Sean 53
Dozier, Brian 26
Dyson, Tyler 103, 113
Eaton, Adam 28
Elías, Roenis 55
Fedde, Erick 57
Freeman, Cole 101, 114
Fuentes, Steven 103, 112
Garcia, Luis 90, 106
Gomes, Yan 30
Guerra, Javy 60
Harper, Ryne 62
Harris, Will 64
Hellickson, Jeremy 66
Hernandez, David 103
Hernandez, Yadiel 101
Hudson, Daniel 68
Kendrick, Howie 32
Kieboom, Carter 91, 105
Kieboom, Spencer 101
McGowin, Kyle 70
Mendoza, Drew 101, 109
Noll, Jake 92
Parra, Gerardo 34
Pena, Viandel 101, 114
Pineda, Israel 101, 111
Rainey, Tanner 72
Raquet, Nick 113
Read, Raudy 93
Reynolds, Matt 101
Robles, Victor 36
Rodney, Fernando 74
Romero, Seth 99, 109
Ross, Joe 76
Rutledge, Jackson 100, 106
Sanchez, Adrian 101
Sánchez, Aníbal 86
Scherzer, Max 78
Sharp, Sterling 111
Sipp, Tony 103
Soto, Juan 38
Stevenson, Andrew 94

Washington Nationals 2020

Strasburg, Stephen 80
Strickland, Hunter 82
Suero, Wander 84
Suzuki, Kurt 41
Taylor, Michael A. 95
Tetreault, Jackson 114
Thames, Eric 43
Turner, Trea 45
Venters, Jonny 103
Voth, Austin 88
Williams, Austen 103
Yean, Eddy 103, 110
Zimmerman, Ryan 47